WALKING IN ITALY'S STELVIO NATIONAL PARK

About the Author

Gillian Price was born in England but moved to Australia when young. After taking a degree in anthropology and working in adult education, she set off to travel through Asia and trek the Himalayas. The culmination of her journey was Venice where, her enthusiasm fired for mountains, the next logical step was towards the Dolomites, only hours away. Starting there, Gillian is steadily exploring the mountain ranges and flatter bits of Italy and bringing them to life for visitors in a series of guides for Cicerone.

When not out walking with Nicola, her Venetian cartographer husband, Gillian works as a freelance travel writer (www.gillianprice.eu). A strong promoter of public transport to minimise impact in alpine areas, she is an active member of the Italian Alpine Club CAI and Mountain Wilderness.

Other Cicerone guides by the author

WALKING IN ITALY'S STELVIO NATIONAL PARK

by Gillian Price

2 POLICE SQUARE, MILNTHORPE, CUMBRIA LA7 7PY
www.cicerone.co.uk

© Gillian Price 2013
First edition 2013
ISBN: 978 1 85284 690 9

Printed in China on behalf of Latitude Press Ltd.
A catalogue record for this book is available from the British Library.

Maps by Nicola Regine.
Photographs by the author.

Dedication

For dear Nicola – companion, sherpa and mapmaker par excellence

Acknowledgments

Thanks to Chris and Steve as well as the Madden family for their enthusiastic company, and to Massimo Favaron and Enrico Bassi of the Stelvio National Park for their inspiration.

Advice to Readers

While every effort is made by our authors to ensure the accuracy of guide-books as they go to print, changes can occur during the lifetime of an edition. If we know of any, there will be an Updates tab on this book's page on the Cicerone website (www.cicerone.co.uk), so please check before planning your trip. We also advise that you check information about such things as transport, accommodation and shops locally. Even rights of way can be altered over time. We are always grateful for information about any discrepancies between a guidebook and the facts on the ground, sent by email to information@cicerone.co.uk or by post to Cicerone, 2 Police Square, Milnthorpe LA7 7PY, United Kingdom.

Front cover: The dramatic setting of Trafoi on the Südtirol approach to the famous Stelvio Pass (Walks 27 and 28)

CONTENTS

Warning

Mountain walking can be a dangerous activity carrying a risk of personal injury or death. It should be undertaken only by those with a full understanding of the risks and with the training and experience to evaluate them. While every care and effort has been taken in the preparation of this guide, the user should be aware that conditions can be highly variable and can change quickly, materially affecting the seriousness of a mountain walk. Therefore, except for any liability which cannot be excluded by law, neither Cicerone nor the author accept liability for damage of any nature (including damage to property, personal injury or death) arising directly or indirectly from the information in this book.

To call out the Mountain Rescue ring 118 – this will connect you via any available network. Once connected ask for *soccorso alpino*.

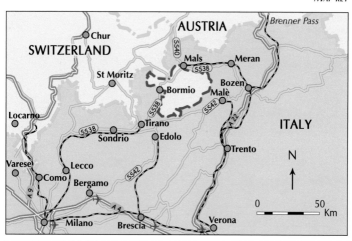

Map key

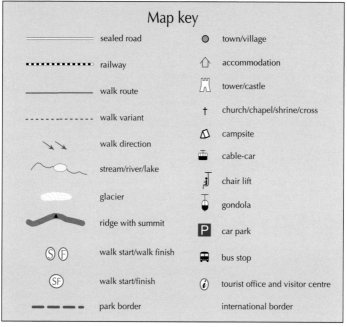

——————— sealed road	● town/village
▪▪▪▪▪▪▪▪▪▪ railway	⌂ accommodation
——— walk route	🏰 tower/castle
- - - - - walk variant	† church/chapel/shrine/cross
↘↘ walk direction	◊ campsite
～⬭～ stream/river/lake	🚡 cable-car
⬭ glacier	🚡 chair lift
▬▬▲▬▬ ridge with summit	🚠 gondola
Ⓢ Ⓕ walk start/walk finish	🅿 car park
㊋ walk start/finish	🚌 bus stop
– – – – park border	ⓘ tourist office and visitor centre
	international border

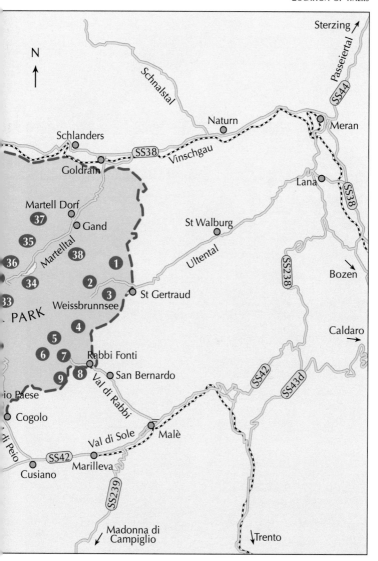

N ↑

Sterzing ↗

Passeiertal

SS44

Schnalstal

Naturn

Meran

Schlanders

SS38

Vinschgau

Goldrain

Lana

SS38

Martell Dorf

37

Gand

St Walburg

35

Martelltal

38

1

Ultental

SS238

Bozen

36

34

2

33

3

St Gertraud

PARK

Weissbrunnsee

Caldaro →

4

5

6

7

Rabbi Fonti

9

8

San Bernardo

SS42

SS43d

io Paese

Val di Rabbi

Cogolo

Val di Sole

Malè

di Peio

SS42

Marilleva

Cusiano

SS239

Madonna di
Campiglio ↙

↓Trento

9

The breathtaking views from Hintergrathütte (Walk 30)

INTRODUCTION

The mountainous Stelvio National Park, established in 1935, lies due west of the Dolomites in northeast Italy. The most extensive Italian alpine park, it sprawls for 1300 square kilometres across the heart of the Central Alps, embracing a wilderness of rugged glaciated summits and ridges and culminating in the massive 3905m Ortler. In between run beautiful verdant valleys cloaked with dense forests, home to both traditional village settlements and welcoming well-equipped resorts. Visitors can choose from dozens of exciting walks, each with the guarantee of breathtaking landscapes, wildflowers and wildlife day after day after day.

This guide gives a selection of routes from each of the major valleys, presenting walks across the full range of difficulties and from a couple of hours to a full day in length. Also included are spectacular non-glacier summits that are accessible to walkers who want to go that bit further (Walks 11, 19, 23, 25, 32 and 37).

GEOGRAPHY

The alpine landscape in the Stelvio National Park has been shaped by the massive glaciers which covered the area as long as 7000 years ago. In winter they are fed by snow, which compresses into ice, the accumulated

Vast panoramas towards the Forni glacier and Pizzo Tresero can be enjoyed (Walk 21)

weight dragging the glaciers down-hill. When the rate of summer melting exceeds that of maintaining the status quo, the ice mass reduces in volume and retreats to higher ground where temperatures are lower, often leaving behind a typical U-shaped trough. Moreover, clumps of *roches moutonnées* are commonly found on vast rock surfaces that have been left exposed, smoothed by the passage of ice and grooved by stones trapped underneath the glacier and dragged along.

Other rock debris plucked off mountain flanks ends up on top of the slowly moving body of ice. Over time it rattles off to the sides in elongated rows known as moraine. When the glacier withdraws, these remain in place and are colonised by pioneer plants such as mountain avens,

which consolidate the terrain, leading the way for cushion vegetation then shrubs.

As is happening across the whole of the Alps, the Stelvio's glaciers are shrinking rapidly and over the last 50 years 40% of the total surface area – equivalent to 20 sq km – has been lost (21% alone over the period 1991–2003).

HISTORY

Before World War I, east of Switzerland the border between Italy and the Austro-Hungarian Empire extended as far south as Lake Garda and Trento. In 1915, after signing a secret treaty with the Triple Entente of the UK, France and Russia, Italy entered WWI, declaring war on its

Italian WWI observatory on the Filone dei Möt ridge (Walk 25)

former ally and neighbour and opening a new, urgently needed front. The fledgling Kingdom (which came into existence in 1860) had been promised the extension of its border north to the Brenner Pass as well as Istria. Troops were sent to dig in along the northeastern Italian Alps, high-altitude mountains beset with glaciers and snowed in for five months of the year. Vast labyrinths of ice tunnels spelled protection – along with disconcerting creaking as the glacier moved and sub-zero temperatures prevailed. As things turned out, there was relatively little action; however, the harsh conditions and avalanches caused shocking loss of life. When the war ended with the 1918 Treaty of Versailles the Südtirol (South Tyrol) became Italy's Alto Adige.

Many of the old mule tracks and military supply roads form the basis for today's walking routes. In this guidebook Walks 11–14, 19, 20, 23–26 and 29 follow such routes or visit WWI sites, poignant places that testify to the folly of man. Nowadays the magnificent landscapes can be enjoyed in the peace of a united Europe.

NOMENCLATURE

The Stelvio National Park stretches over the Italian regions of Südtirol, Trentino and Lombardia. In the first, the German language is dominant (spoken by 80% of the inhabitants) and although all the place names were translated into Italian after 1918,

in this guide the original German names have been given preference, as they are generally more meaningful in situ (the Italian version is provided when mentioned the first time). Although all road and place signs are bilingual, it can be a bit confusing: for instance, the famous road pass known as Stilfser Joch (or Stilfserjoch) in German is the Passo dello Stelvio for the Italians. Refuges changed hands postwar, spawning a gallery of double names such as Düsseldorferhütte–Rifugio Serristori.

PLANTS AND FLOWERS

Thanks to the variety of terrains and habitats it encompasses – from low-lying meadows through woods and scrub to high-altitude rock and icescapes – the Stelvio offers an incredible range of alpine plant life and some interesting examples of adaptation to harsh environments.

The vast forests cloaking mid-altitude slopes are mostly conifer, dominated by the Arolla pine. This relies on the industrious nutcracker for its survival, as the voracious – and forgetful – bird hoards kernels in secluded rock crannies where the trees sprout and grow. Another coniferous tree seen throughout the park is the larch, which has lacy fronds; it is the only conifer to lose its needles in autumn. Its common companions are bushes of miniature rhododendrons or alpenrose with pink blooms, a delight in July. Scree slopes, on the other hand,

1) Autumn gentian; 2) Gorgeous tiny gentians; 3) Leopard's bane

are colonised by the hardy dwarf mountain pine, with springy branches that trap the snow.

Seemingly barren rock surfaces host myriad coloured lichen, which prepare the surface for hardy cushion plants such as the efficient 'rock breaker' saxifrage, with penetrating roots and tiny delicate blooms. Among the first flowers to appear on the edge of the snow line is the dainty fringed blue-violet alpine snowbell. The heat it releases as it breaks down carbohydrates actually melts the snow. Another early bloom is the perfumed sticky primrose, with petite clusters of deep purple. A lover of siliceous scree, the white or rarer pink glacier crowfoot

grows close to glaciers, hence its name. The leaf cells contain a rich fluid that acts as an antifreeze.

Elsewhere, stony grasslands with calcareous soil (from limestone or dolomite) are ideal for delicate, sweet-scented yellow Rhaetian poppies. Often found growing nearby are white star-shaped edelweiss, their leaves equipped with fine felt-like hairs which trap heat. Rocky terrain is also the home of the gentian, which comes as a gorgeous blue trumpet or tiny iridescent stars; there is also a showy yellow-spotted type and delicate mauve varieties in autumn. Eye-catching alpine moon daisies are a common sight on rock-strewn slopes, which they share with clumps of golden leopard's bane and spidery creeping avens. Common alongside marshy lakes is fluffy white cotton grass, while purple or white insectivorous butterwort is found in damp places, often near streams. Pasture slopes and alpine meadows straight out of *The Sound of Music* are dotted with exquisite wine-red martagon lilies, delicate columbines and the tiny triangular-headed black vanilla orchids, which smell of cocoa. Flower picking is of course strictly forbidden.

A valuable aid to identification is *Alpine Flowers of Britain and Europe* by C Grey-Wilson and M Blamey (Collins: 2nd edition, 2001); sadly, this is now out of print but is occasionally available second hand. The Rezia Alpine Botanical Garden in Bormio has labelled species and is open in summer.

WILDLIFE

Many birds and animals that live at high altitudes have developed thick furry coats and plumage which even cover their legs and the contours of their beaks. Small air bubbles captured between the hairs or feathers can generate a layer of insulation that helps reduce heat loss.

One of the easiest animals for walkers to see is the alpine marmot. These furry beaver-like creatures live in burrow colonies on grass-rock terrain and hibernate from October to April. In summer they forage for sugary wildflowers, dashing back to safety when warned of danger by

Majestic ibex dwell happily throughout the Stelvio

the shrill cry of a sentry. The widespread conifer woods provide shelter for roe deer and stately red deer, shy creatures best seen at dusk. They often leave hoof prints in the mud. Less intimidated by human presence are the magnificent ibex, which sport sturdy grooved horns – in males these can grow as long as 1m. Their hooves have a fold in the skin which allows them to grip the rocks. Reintroduced back in the 1960s, they happily dwell throughout the Stelvio. The highest mountain dweller of the ruminants is the fleet-footed chamois. A mountain goat with short curved horns like crochet hooks, it can be seen in herds clambering nimbly on impossibly steep cliffs.

Sightings of the brown bear have increased significantly in the area over the last few years. They wander into

The common viper has a distinct diamond pattern on its back

Alpine marmots colonise the grass-rock terrain

the Stelvio from neighbouring alpine regions in search of food, often causing alarm in villages where people are no longer used to their presence. To date, however, there is no evidence they have actually taken up residence in the park.

There is a fair chance you may encounter a viper on paths, as these cold-blooded reptiles need to sun themselves. With a light grey-brown body and triangular head, the snakes grow to around 70–80cm long and can be distinguished by the elegant markings on their back: diamond-patterned in the case of the common viper (*Vipera berus*) or dark streaks for the rarer asp viper (*Vipera aspis*). They live on small rodents, which they swallow whole and take time digesting. Timid creatures, they will flee if surprised and only attack out of self-defence, so give them time to slither away as they will probably be lethargic. While their bite does contain venom, this is rarely fatal to humans (small children and the elderly are most at risk). In the unlikely event that someone is bitten, seek help immediately and keep the victim still and calm. Learn to identify a viper and distinguish it from non-venomous snakes.

Birdwatchers will enjoy the sight of crag martins skimming alpine meadows and lakes in search of insects. Arolla pine forests, meanwhile, are the favourite habitat of the dappled, aptly named nutcracker, expert at cracking open pine nuts with its thick beak. From a perch at the top of the tree they also act as lookouts, their piercing squawk a clear warning for other inhabitants of the wood of potential danger. Higher up are alpine choughs, elegant crows with glossy black wings and yellow beaks; they perform entertaining aerial displays of acrobatics to the accompaniment of a noisy, chattering commentary. Choughs have the incredible knack of appearing out of nowhere at the mere rustle of a picnic bag, to beg for crumbs.

On a larger scale are birds of prey such as kites, buzzards and the superb golden eagle, which has a wingspan that can reach 2.2m. These prey on small mammals such as hares and young marmots, but will also take birds. In winter the eagle has been known to scavenge the carcasses of animals such as chamois which have fallen victim to avalanches. This puts it in direct competition with the recently returned bearded vulture or Lammergeier, which also keeps an eye out for migrating birds which drop from exhaustion as they fly through the lower alpine passes in springtime on their way north. With a wingspan up to 2.8m, a body over 1m long and weighing in at 5–7kg, the bearded vulture is easily recognised, especially as its eyesight is poor so it often flies close to the ground. Its diet is composed of 80% bones, which it cracks open by dropping them from a height onto rocks. Successfully reintroduced across the Alps, it has made its home in the park. Check out the webcam in a nest in Val Zebrù: www.gipetostelvio.it is reality TV like you have never seen before.

Wildlife lovers will especially enjoy Martelltal, Val Zebrù and Valle di Rabbi, where there are lots of animals that are relatively easy to spot. A final note: injured creatures are nursed back to recovery in the *area faunistica* (wildlife area) at Peio Fonti. Here visitors have better chances of seeing deer and other ruminants than out in the wild.

One excellent guidebook is the *Birds of Britain and Europe* by B Bruun, H Delin and L Svensson (Hamlyn, 1992).

VALLEYS AND BASES

We begin with the eastern section of the Stelvio National Park in Südtirol. A short way south of Meran/Merano

Traditional timber farms in Ultental

is Lana, where Ultental/Val d'Ultimo breaks off southwest. A world apart – inhabited by descendants of migrants from a monastery in German Swabia – it is a rare traditional valley of great allure. The mountainsides are dotted with clusters of timber chalets and barns crafted with bulky tree trunks intricately notched together. Stained red with age, they stand witness to the valley's agricultural heritage. All around extend manicured emerald meadows, on impossibly steep slopes where mowers must be fitted with spikes to enable farmers to harvest the hay without slipping. Pastoral activities have been key to the economy since as early as the 17th century, when 20,000 sheep were sent to graze from as far afield as Verona. Vast forests of larch and pine provide shelter to both red and roe deer, and feed the sawmills of the flourishing timber industry.

The tourist office, supermarket and ATM are located at St Walburg/Santa Valburga, about halfway up the valley. The highest village is St Gertraud/Santa Geltrude. Served all year round by SAD buses, it is the start of Walk 1. There is a grocery shop, café-restaurant, a scattering of hotels and a centuries-old Venetian-style sawmill driven by water. Fully operational until the 1980s, the Lahnersäge now doubles as a Park Information Point. A stroll away stand the Urlärchen, three ancient larch trees that have been there for over 2000 years. A trifle battered and damaged by lightning strikes, they are still the oldest conifers in the whole of Europe. The road ends further uphill at Weissbrunnsee/Lago

On the Saent waterfall route in Val di Rabbi (Walk 7)

Fontana Bianca (Walks 2 and 3), one of the many lakes dammed in the 1960s for hydroelectricity to capture the glacier melt.

Forming the southernmost edge of the Stelvio National Park, Val di Sole lies wholly within the Italian-speaking region of Trentino. Although *sole* means 'sun' in Italian, the name is derived from the Celtic goddess of waters, found in abundance here. It runs due west–east from Passo del Tonale beneath glaciated ranges and alongside apple orchards. Malè is the key railway station (FTM Ferrovia Trento Malè trains from Trento to Marilleva), while all the district's bus services (Trentino Trasporti) fan out from here. Its charming historic centre hosts markets, a wealth of gourmet food shops, hotels, ATMs and a tourist office.

Two beautiful side valleys branch north off Val di Sole; both correspond to geological faults and are rich in mineral waters (a bottling plant operates at Peio). Mining was once widespread, and traces of the activity live on in place names such as Fucine, meaning 'furnace'.

Val di Rabbi forks north from Malè. San Bernardo is the first sizeable village with tourist information and an ATM, as well as hotels. Not far along is the low-key spa resort of Rabbi Fonti (with a Park Visitor Centre and hotels), the end of the bus line and the perfect base for Walks 4–9. The attractions of this lovely valley – free from ski infrastructure – include the fascinating Segheria Veneziana sawmill, the spectacular Saent waterfalls, the varied wildlife and the active dairy farms that play an important

19

Peio Fonti spa resort (Walks 11–13)

part in the economy. Summer shuttle buses organised by the National Park serve the side valleys.

Val di Peio, or Pejo, forks north-west off the Val di Sole at Cusiano. A string of old alpine communities that thrive on tourism and a mineral water bottling plant are centred around Cogolo (Park Visitor Centre, ATM). Here the valley forks – north leads up the narrowing thickly forested valley to Malga Mare, gateway to a refuge set opposite the Cevedale and cascading glaciers (Walk 10).

The other fork goes west to Peio Fonti, a renowned spa resort that makes a first-rate base for walkers, with a jumble of hotels, groceries, ATM and cable car. Walks 11–13 are accessed from here, including spectacular Monte Vioz. Buses from Malè serve Peio Fonti before continuing up to the pretty village of Peio Paese, a peaceful spot perched on the sunny hillside with lovely views, food shops and accommodation. Its 15th-century bell tower boasts a remarkable 7m tall fresco portraying St Christopher. A minor road proceeds west along Val del Monte (Walk 14) as far as Fontanino di Celentino (Walk 15).

Located in Alta Valtellina, the bustling alpine township of Bormio is an excellent starting point for visiting the western Lombardia slice of the Stelvio National Park. It has a charming centre with medieval buildings that testify to the town's strategic importance at an alpine crossroads, and in winter people flock here for the extensive ski domain. There is a decent range of accommodation and facilities (supermarkets, ATM, park and tourist information). Bormio is

The famous Stelvio road on the Südtirol side

easily reached by public transport: Perego buses are plentiful from Tirano (on the rail line from Milano as well as St Moritz in Switzerland and the spectacular Bernina Express). At a sunny confluence of valleys, it is dominated by a striking limestone crest, Reit. Bormio is handy for Walk 23; moreover, the dramatic Stelvio Pass road strikes out north close to the Swiss border, providing access for Walks 24 and 25.

Branching east from Bormio is Valfurva; here the village of San Nicolò marks the opening of wild and wonderful Val Zebrù, explored in Walk 20. From there it is a very short trip to the resort village of Santa Caterina Valfurva (bus, hotels, groceries, ATM, tourist information) and Walks 16 and 21. A convenient base in itself, it acts as the gateway to Valle

dei Forni and Val Cedèc, which offer high-altitude refuges and magnificent glaciers. At their confluence stands historic Rifugio Forni, a wonderful place to stay, especially if you plan on Walks 17, 18 and 21.

Entry to the northeast section of the National Park is via Südtirol's Vinschgau/Val Venosta, home to the handy Meran–Mals train that runs through apple orchards. At Spondinig/Spondigna a road heads southwest to the junction of Gomagoi. Here Suldental/Val di Solda slices south to the sun-blessed resort of Sulden/Solda, which offers a host of hotels, a tourist office, ATM, supermarket, year-round SAD buses, chairlifts and a cable car. The spectacular presence of the glaciated giants Ortler and Königspitze make every outing here breathtaking – Walks 29–31.

21

From Gomagoi the road continues southwest up Trafoiertal/Valle di Trafoi, steep-sided, narrow and edged by a stunning line-up of glaciers and soaring peaks – the setting for Trafoi (Walks 27 and 28). This tiny village serves the great Stelvio Pass, and is the destination of the road and the summer SAD buses. In winter when the road is closed the village's 80 residents enjoy peace and quiet with no through traffic. The name comes from the ancient Ladin language spoken by the original inhabitants. Sources link the meaning with 'clover' or 'three springs', in view of the much-visited Drei Brunnen sanctuary nearby (Walk 28). It is home to the 1970s Italian ski champion Gustav Thöni of 'Valanga Azzurra' ('blue avalanche') fame. It has an ATM, groceries, a fair sprinkling of hotels as well as a camping ground and well-run visitor information centre.

Martelltal/Val Martello turns south off Vinschgau and the train line at Goldrain/Coldrano, not far from Latsches/Laces (tourist office). This magnificent unspoilt alpine valley is a superb introduction to the nature and glacial environment of the Stelvio National Park and it has a good scattering of hotels and guesthouses. The lower–mid reaches are occupied by thriving settlements of shepherds and farmers who have branched out into growing strawberries, while further up the slopes are heavily wooded and home to deer and chamois. A great bonus is the absence of bulldozed ski slopes and lifts.

Year-round SAD buses run via Gand to the lively village of Martell Dorf/Martello (shops and ATM). Here a side road goes on to terminate at the renowned family-run Stallwieshof and start of Walk 37 to Orgelspitze.

From Gand a summer extension serves the upper valley via Waldheim (Walk 38) as far as Gasthof Enzian. This cosy establishment makes an excellent base for Walks 32–36, which wander up paths to natural belvederes taking in waterfalls and glaciers in the shadow of the majestic Cevedale.

GETTING THERE

By plane
Handy airports are located at Milano (Linate and Malpensa www.sea-aeroportimilano.it), Bergamo (Orio Al Serio www.sacbo.it) and Brescia (www.aeroportobrescia.it) for the western valleys of Lombardia, while Verona (www.aeroportoverona.it) is better placed for accessing the Trentino and Südtirol sections. Innsbruck airport (www.innsbruck-airport.com) is useful if approaching from Austria and the north.

By train
From Milano Centrale, Trenitalia trains run via Lecco then along the Valtellina to Tirano, which doubles as the terminus for the Bernina Express from St Moritz in Switzerland. From Brescia, the Trenord railway via Iseo goes as far as Edolo. The main Verona–Brenner

Approaching the Torri di Fraele and Monte delle Scale (Walk 23)

Pass line served by Trenitalia is good for Trento, where the FTM branch line heads off to Malè. Further north is Bozen/Bolzano where a line forks off for Meran/Merano and from there Vinschgau/Val Venosta and the terminal of Mals/Malles. Travellers arriving from Austria on the Brenner Pass line can use either Trenitalia or Austrian Rail.

By road

Via Europe's extensive network of motorways, useful entry points to Italy for the Stelvio National Park are from Austria via the Brenner Pass and the A22 *autostrada* (motorway), or via Landeck through the Reschenpass. From Switzerland the Umbrail and Bernina passes will be open in summer, otherwise there is the A9 via Como to Milano.

LOCAL TRANSPORT

It is perfectly feasible to have a car-free holiday in the Stelvio National Park, and thus avoid contributing to air pollution and congestion. An excellent, extensive and reasonably priced network of trains and buses serves villages and valleys across the three regions and nearly all the walks in this guidebook start and finish at places accessible by public transport. This means that the driving is done by experts who know the roads and hairpin bends like the back of their hand, leaving passengers free to sit back and enjoy the magnificent scenery. Where there is no bus, a local taxi is usually available. Strategically placed cable cars and chairlifts are also used on several walks to facilitate ascents.

23

In Lombardia Perego buses start out from Tirano railway station and serve Bormio and the surroundings areas with Passo dello Stelvio (Stilfser Joch). The company also has a link from Edolo via Aprica to Tirano.

In Südtirol SAD trains link Meran with Mals, and from the intermediate stations buses run up the Ultental, Martelltal, Suldental and Trafoiertal, extending to the Stilfser Joch (Passo dello Stelvio).

The Trentino valleys are served by Trentino Trasporti trains from Trento to Malè with connecting buses to the Rabbi and Peio valleys.

Bus tickets should usually be purchased in advance, either at the bus station or at newsstands or tobacconists displaying the appropriate logo.

Generally speaking, summer timetables cover the June to September period, but this tends to vary from year to year and place to place. Local tourist offices are always in the know and timetables can be consulted on the websites listed in Appendix D. Several good deals are available for visitors – always enquire locally. Alta Valtellina has an excellent value 'Welcome Card' for the Perego bus networks. In Südtirol, 'Mobilcard'

USEFUL EXPRESSIONS

The following expressions may come in useful when purchasing tickets.

Un biglietto/due biglietti per Malè per favore	One ticket/two tickets to Malè please
Andata	single
Andata e ritorno	return
Quanto costa?	How much is that?
Grazie	Thank you
Prego	You're welcome

The following phrases may be helpful for understanding timetables.

Cambio a…/coincidenza	change at…/connection
Estivo/invernale	summer/winter
Feriale	working days (Monday to Saturday)
Festivo	holidays (Sundays and public holidays)
Giornaliero	daily
Lunedì a venerdì/sabato	Monday to Friday/Saturday
Navetta	shuttle service
Sciopero	strike
Scolastico	during school term

The Ortler is seen beyond the chairlift (Walk 26)

multi-day passes are recommended for the SAD lines; a multi-trip ticket 'carta valori' is also on sale.

Contact details for bus, train, local taxi, cable car and chairlift companies are listed in Appendix D.

INFORMATION

The Italian Tourist Board has offices all over the world and can help prospective travellers with general information (see www.enit.it).

UK: 1 Princes St, London W1B 2AY Tel 207 3993562.

USA: 630, Fifth Avenue – suite 1656, New York NY 10111 Tel 212 2455618.

Australia: Level 4, 46 Market St, Sydney, NSW 2000 Tel 02 92621666.

The many tourist offices in the Stelvio valleys can provide help with local accommodation and transport (see contact details in Appendix D). When making a phone call in Italy, remember to always include the initial zero of the landline number. Numbers beginning with '3' are mobiles and need to be dialled as they stand (in other words without a zero). If calling from overseas preface all Italian telephone numbers with +39.

The Stelvio National Park websites are www.stelviopark.it and www.parks.it/parco.nazionale.stelvio. Visitor Centres are open throughout the midsummer months. All have a summer calendar of guided walks which visitors can join for a very modest fee. See Appendix D for contact details.

WHEN TO GO

The best time to visit Stelvio is July, August and September when the walking days are long, conditions are good, and facilities such as refuges and local transport are readily available. However, as early as June, low to mid-altitude paths will often be snow-free, flowers will be starting to bloom and hotels offer off-season rates. October can mean crystal clear skies, perfect visibility and autumn colours, although there is a risk of early snow. Italy goes off summer daylight saving

25

time at the end of October, giving shorter days for walking.

ACCOMMODATION

Villages and towns throughout the Stelvio National Park offer a good range of hotel (*albergo*), guesthouse (*locanda, Gasthof*), bed and breakfast (*affittacamera, Garni,* B&B) and farm stay (*agriturismo*) accommodation to suit all pockets. Suggestions are given in Appendix C. Families with small children will appreciate the freedom of a house (*casa*) or flat (*appartamento*); rentals are common, usually on a weekly basis – consult the relevant tourist office website.

Reservation – even in key resorts such as Sulden/Solda or Bormio – is not usually necessary outside the mid-August peak season, but it is always best to book ahead to avoid disappointment. If you are driving through, look out for signs saying *camera libera* (Italian) or *Zimmer frei* (German) signs.

Camping and overnight bivouacs are strictly forbidden within the Stelvio National Park, except in emergencies. A tent is still a good option for a low-budget holiday but be aware that campsites are few and far between – see Appendix C for listings.

Although all the walks described in this guidebook are designed to be completed in a single day to allow for a return to valley accommodation, an overnight stay in a high-altitude alpine *rifugio* (refuge) is always a memorable experience and can be the highlight of a walking holiday. With the odd

Approaching Tabarettahütte (Walk 29)

exception at road level, these refuges are located in spectacular high-altitude positions accessible only on foot. They are generally open from late June to late September/October (although a handful open in spring for ski tourers).

Refuges offer reasonably priced meals and refreshments as well as sleeping facilities that range from spartan dormitories with bunk beds to cosy simple guest rooms. Pillows and blankets are always provided so sleeping bags are not needed. Sleeping sheets are, however, compulsory in club huts so carry your own. You will also need a small towel. Flip-flops or lightweight rubber sandals are a good idea as boots are not worn inside huts. Hut rules also include no smoking and lights out from 10pm–6am. Charges are around €18–25 for a bed and €40–50 for half board, which means a three-course dinner, overnight stay and breakfast. Some huts are privately owned, although the majority belong to the Italian Alpine Club CAI (Club Alpino Italiano), its Trentino branch SAT (Società Alpinisti Tridentini) and the Südtirol Club AVS (Alpenverein Südtirol).

Refuges – whether club or privately managed – are open to everyone. Members of affiliated alpine associations from other countries get discounted rates (approximately 50% off bed rates) in line with reciprocal agreements. Members of the British Mountaineering Council and Mountaineering Council of Scotland can buy a Reciprocal Rights Card from the BMC website (www.thebmc. co.uk), and it is also possible to join the UK branch of the Austrian Alpine Club (Tel 01929 556870; www.aacuk. org.uk) or CAI, the Italian Alpine Club (www.cai.it) – contact an individual branch directly.

Refuge accommodation must be booked in advance on July and August weekends, preferably by phone as few have email access during the summer. 'Vorrei prenotare un posto letto/ due posti letto' means 'I'd like to book one/two beds'. Be aware that if you book but do not turn up, you could set in motion costly (for you!) alpine search and rescue procedures, so remember to phone and cancel if you change your plans; but do give plenty of warning for courtesy. Some establishments accept credit cards but it is best to carry a supply of euros in cash to be on the safe side. See Appendix C for listings of all the refuges visited in this guide.

FOOD AND DRINK

A holiday in the Stelvio National Park is also a guarantee of memorable gastronomical experiences thanks to the rich culinary traditions of the Lombardia, Trentino and Südtirol regions.

Hearty soups feature regularly on menus: *minestrone* with vegetables is unfailingly satisfying, as is substantial *zuppa d'orzo* with barley, while *Gulaschsuppe*, a rich tomatoey soup with chunks of beef and paprika, is another good bet. Pasta starts with *pizzoccheri*, a wholesome and filling

Lyfi Alm provides home-style meals and refreshments (Walk 35)

dish of buckwheat pasta, cabbage and potatoes smothered with melted cheese. *Gnocchi con ortiche* are tiny potato and nettle dumplings, while Trentino versions are *strangolapreti* (priest stranglers!) incorporating spinach, and *monchi* made with polenta (cornmeal) and smothered with sage-flavoured butter. Do try *capelazzi*, over-sized ravioli stuffed with ricotta, and when in the Südtirol, if you can get your tongue around the name, seek out *Kartoffelteigtaschen mit Bergkäse*, pockets of fresh pasta filled with soft potato and served with melted local cheese.

A *tagliere* ('cutting board'/platter) is always a good choice for lunch or a snack, especially at a mountain farm or eatery with local dairy products, and will hold a selection of local cheeses,

cold meats and sausage served with bread. In the Trentino valleys *Casolet* is a guarantee of a smooth, tasty cow's cheese made using a traditional technique. *Poina* is a sort of ricotta (a non-lumpy version of cottage cheese), a creamy fresh spread produced with whey and either smeared on bread with *miele* (honey), or melted over hot polenta (cornmeal). Another version is Asni, which has garlic, salt and pepper added before being *enfumegada* (smoked) to keep it longer. There are plenty of cold sausages similar to salami. Valtellina is renowned for its *Bresaola*, dried beef flavoured with juniper berries and herbs and eaten in transparent slices. The area's cheese production is prodigious – *scumid* is a sharp type and goat's cheese (*formaggio di capra*) is common, both fresh as

Kaiserschmarrn, a Südtirol speciality

well as compact, pungent and mature. *Sciatt* (literally 'toad' in dialect) are delicious cheese-filled fritters made with grappa-flavoured batter.

Of the vast choice of meats, spicy goulash stew and *stinco* or roast pork shank are dishes to look forward to.

On the sweet front, in the Trentino valleys look out for carrot cakes (*torta di carote*) or the variously spelled *torta di fregoloti*, a delectable lumpy shortbread made with chopped almonds. In the Südtirol go for either *Kaiserschmarrn*, a concoction of sliced pancake with dried fruit and redcurrant jelly, or the ubiquitous *Apfelstrudel* (sliced apple enveloped in thin filo-like pastry) sold in every bakery, pastry shop and café.

As regards liquid refreshment, homemade cordials may be on offer such as *Holunder* (elderflower) or even alpenrose. There is a range of high-quality wines – all reds – from the valleys surrounding the Stelvio Park: Lagrein and Blauburgunder from the Bozen basin, Teroldego and Schiava from the Trentino valleys, and fragrant Sassella and Inferno from Valtellina.

Coffee comes in classical Italian style with short black *espresso*, milky frothy *cappuccino* or less concentrated *caffé latte*.

Most villages and farms still have their age-old drinking fountains. Tap water (*acqua da rubinetto*) is always safe to drink (*potabile* means drinkable) and can be requested in cafés and restaurants instead of the bottled mineral water that causes so much unnecessary pollution as it is transported back and forth across Europe.

29

WHAT TO TAKE

- Good quality waterproof boots with ankle support and non-slip soles, preferably not brand new unless you plan to protect your feet with sticking plaster. Trainers are inadequate for alpine paths.
- A comfortable medium-sized rucksack (max 20 litres capacity), large enough to contain food, drink and necessities for a full day out.
- Rain gear – a waterproof jacket, trousers and rucksack cover are ideal, or a full-length poncho; a folding umbrella is handy for walkers who wear glasses.
- Binoculars for watching birds and animals, and a camera.
- A basic first aid kit including sticking plasters.
- Maps, compass and altimeter.
- A whistle and headlamp or torch for attracting attention in emergencies.
- Sun hat, glasses and high-factor suncream; remember that for every 1000m of ascent, the intensity of the sun's UV rays increases by 10%, and many walks in this guidebook are above the tree line.
- A range of layered clothing to cater for conditions ranging from fiery sun through to lashing rain and storms, and occasionally snow.
- Lightweight telescopic trekking poles are handy for descending steep slopes and easing the weight of a rucksack off knees and back.
- A full day's supply of water. At some huts the water may be labelled *non potabile* (undrinkable) if supplies come from snow-melt. Check with the staff if in doubt.
- Although food is available at huts on the majority of walks described here, it is best not to rely on them – always be self-sufficient and carry generous amounts of your own. Bad weather, minor accidents and all manner of unforeseen factors could hold you up on the track, and that extra biscuit or energy bar could become crucial.
- Mineral salt tablets are helpful in combating salt depletion and dehydration caused by profuse sweating; unexplained prolonged fatigue and symptoms similar to heatstroke indicate a problem.

MAPS

The Stelvio National Park has an excellent network of paths, each marked with frequently placed red/white paint stripes on prominent fence posts, tree trunks and rocks, and complete with its own distinguishing number. Note that path numbers were recently changed across the park in line with a nationwide campaign to standardise waymarking. The old faded numbers are still visible on the ground in places, although new ones

Waymarking on a tree trunk

appear on signposts and updated editions of maps so there should be no cause for confusion.

Sketch maps are provided in this guidebook showing the layout of the walk, with essential landmarks. Limitations of space make it impossible to include full details – essential in an emergency – so it is imperative that walkers obtain a commercial map. The Tabacco 'carta topografica per escursionisti' 1:25,000 scale series is one of the clearest on the market (www.tabaccoeditrice.com). These maps use a continuous red line for a wide track, while a broken red line indicates a marked path of average difficulty. Red dots denote routes that are exposed, difficult or faint, while red crosses denote aided sections such as cable or ladders as well as full-blooded via ferrata routes.

The relevant sheets are:
- N.08 Ortles-Cevedale Ortlergebiet for Walks 16–22, 25–31
- N.045 Laces-Val Martello-Silandro for Walks 1–3, 32–38
- N.048 Val di Peio-Val di Rabbi-Val di Sole for Walks 4–15

The maps are sold in shops throughout the Stelvio National Park as well as leading outdoor suppliers and booksellers worldwide. In the UK consult The Map Shop (www.themapshop.co.uk) or Stanfords (www.stanfords.co.uk) if you prefer to purchase them beforehand.

All the walks are covered by Tabacco, with the exception of Walks 23 and 24, for which you need the new Ingenua 1:25,000 scale maps. Parco Nazionale dello Stelvio Sheet 2 covers Walks 16–25 and 27–31. Order

Signposts in Valfurva

from www.cartoguide.it or purchase at Bormio.

Lastly, www.altavaltellina.eu also do 1:25,000 maps at a cheap €1, although the graphics are not always clear and route difficulty is not shown.

Kompass also has a good range of walking maps that cover the Stelvio (www.kompass-italia.it).

A note on place names: in the Südtirol region of Italy they are bilingual – German and Italian – on maps, signposts and refuges. Both are used in this guidebook the first time they are mentioned, thereafter the German is given preference as that is the region's dominant language.

There is an Italian–German–English glossary of topographic and other useful terms in Appendix B.

DOS AND DON'TS

It is better to arrive early and dry, than late and wet.

- Find time to get in good shape before setting out on your holiday, as it will maximise your enjoyment. You will appreciate the wonderful scenery more if you are not exhausted, and you will react better in an emergency.

- Do not be overly ambitious – choose itineraries suited to your capabilities. Read the walk description carefully before setting out.

- Always leave word at your hotel of your planned route, or sign the hut register if staying in a rifugio, as this may come in helpful for rescuers.

- Do not set out late and always have extra time up your sleeve to allow for detours due to missing bridges or signposts, and wrong turns. Plan on getting to your destination early in hot weather as afternoon storms are not uncommon. As a general rule, start out early morning to give yourself plenty of daylight.

- Stick with your companions and do not lose sight of them. Remember that the progress of groups matches that of the slowest member.

- Avoid walking in brand new footwear, or you will get blisters; but leave old worn-out boots in the shed as they may prove unsafe on slippery terrain. Choose your footwear carefully.

- Do not overload your rucksack.
- Carry extra protective clothing as well as energy foods for emergency situations. Remember that the temperature drops an average of 6°C for every 1000m you climb.
- Check the weather forecast if possible – tourist offices and hut guardians are always in the know. For the Südtirol see www.suedtirol.information, Trentino has www.meteotrentino.it and Lombardia http://ita.arpa lombardia.it. Never set out on a long route in adverse conditions. Even a broad, level track can become treacherous in bad weather, and high-altitude terrain enveloped in thick mist makes orientation difficult. An altimeter

is useful – when a known altitude (such as that of the refuge) goes up, this means the atmospheric pressure has dropped and the weather could change for the worse.

- Do carry your rubbish back to the valley where it can be disposed of correctly; do not expect hut or park staff to deal with it. Even organic waste such as apple cores and orange peel is best not left lying around as it upsets the diet of animals and birds.
- Be considerate when making a toilet stop. Keep away from watercourses, do not leave unsightly paper lying around and remember that abandoned huts and rock overhangs could serve as life-saving shelter for someone else.
- Collecting flowers, insects or minerals is strictly forbidden, as are fires.

The path draws close to Lago di Pian Palù (Walk 15)

- Learn the international call for help, described in the following section. **DO NOT** rely on your mobile phone as many alpine valleys have no signal. Refuges have landlines and experienced staff can always be relied on in an emergency. In electrical storms, do not shelter under trees or rock overhangs and keep away from metallic fixtures.

- Lastly, do not leave your common sense at home.

EMERGENCIES

For medical matters EU residents need a European Health Insurance Card (EHIC). Holders are entitled to free or subsidised emergency treatment in Italy, which has an excellent national health service. UK residents can apply online at www.dh.gov.uk. Australia similarly has a reciprocal agreement – see www.medicareaustralia.gov.au. Other nationalities should take out suitable insurance. In any case travel insurance for a walking holiday is strongly recommended as costs in the case of rescue and repatriation can be hefty. Members of alpine clubs are usually covered, but do check before you depart.

The following services may be of help should problems arise:
- *Polizia* (police) Tel 113
- Health-related urgencies including *ambulanza* (ambulance) and *soccorso alpino* (mountain rescue) Tel 118
- 'Help!' in Italian is *Aiuto!*, pronounced 'eye-you-tow', and *Zu Hilfe!* in German.

Should help be needed, use the following internationally recognised rescue signals: **six** signals per minute either visual (waving a handkerchief or flashing a torch) or audible (shouting or whistling), repeated after a pause of one minute. The answer is **three** visual or audible signals per minute, to be repeated after a one-minute pause. Anyone who sees or hears a call for help must contact the nearest mountain hut or police station, as quickly as possible.

The hand-signals in the diagram below could be useful for communicating at a distance or with a helicopter.

In Lombardia if you call out Mountain Rescue, let them know your location by referring to the numerical code found on the back of all path signposts.

Help required
Raise both arms above head to form a 'Y'

Help not required
Raise one arm above head and extend the other downward, to form the diagonal of an 'N'

The path above Zufallhütte (Walk 33)

USING THIS GUIDE

The 38 walks in this guide have been selected for their suitability for a wide range of active holidaymakers. There is something for everyone, from easy strolls to strenuous climbs to panoramic peaks for experienced walkers. As each walk has been designed to fit into a single day this means carrying a small rucksack and being able to return to comfortable hotel accommodation at day's end. That said, many walks become even more enjoyable if stretched out over two days, with an overnight stay in a rifugio.

Each walk description is preceded by an information box containing the following essential data:

- **Start**
- **Finish**
- **Distance** – given in both kilometres (km) and miles.
- **Ascent/Descent** – this is important information, as height loss and gain rather than distance indicate the effort required and an ascent/descent factor should be summed to difficulty when planning a day out. A walker of average fitness will usually cover 300m (about 1000ft) in ascent in one hour (100m=328ft).

- **Difficulty**
  - Grade 1 – an easy route on clear tracks and paths, suitable for beginners.
  - Grade 2 – paths across typical mountain terrain, often rocky and with significant ups and downs, where a reasonable level of fitness is preferable.
  - Grade 3 – strenuous, often entailing narrow exposed stretches and drawn-out climbs. Experience and extra care are recommended.

It is extremely important to remember that adverse weather

35

conditions will make any route more arduous. Even a level road can be treacherous if icy.

A handful of walks described in this book have brief stretches across rock faces aided by anchored cable. While they are not strictly climbing routes necessitating special equipment, it is essential to keep away from them in bad weather and if a storm is brewing, as metallic fixtures tend to attract lightning. Avoid two-way traffic on a single stretch of cable as it can be awkward and dangerous to try to pass people. It is common sense to wait until people approaching from the opposite direction have passed before you proceed.

- **Walking time** – this does not include pauses for picnics, admiring views, photos and nature stops, so always add on a good couple of hours when planning your day. Partial timings are also given in the route descriptions for key points during the walk.
- Relevant access information is also given.

In the walk descriptions 'path' is used to mean a narrow pedestrian-only way, 'track' and 'lane' are unsurfaced but vehicle-width, while a 'road' is sealed and open to traffic unless specified otherwise. Compass bearings in route directions are in abbreviated form (N, S, NNW and so on) as are right (R) and left (L). Reference landmarks and places encountered en route are in bold type, and altitude in metres above sea level is given as 'm', not to be confused with minutes (abbreviated as min).

Before the climb steepens, Vedretta Pasquale can be admired (Walk 20)

WALK 1
St Gertraud Alm Route

Start/Finish	Bus stop, St Gertraud
Distance	14.5km (9 miles)
Ascent/Descent	700m
Difficulty	Grade 1–2
Walking time	5hr 10min
Access	St Gertraud is the last stop on the year-round SAD bus run from Meran via Lana up Ultental.

Starting out from St Gertraud, this memorable walk explores the northern flanks of the valley on a series of good paths and farm lanes, and the day becomes a fascinating look into the way of life in this part of the world. (Note: do remember to close all gates behind you as you go.) In the woods en route deer and roe deer are not unusual sights for quiet walkers attentive to sudden movements in the undergrowth.

There is a summer café that serves simple meals towards the end of the walk, at Untere Flatschbergalm, although it is also nice to take a picnic and enjoy it in any of the scenic spots along the way.

From the bus stop at **St Gertraud** (1504m), turn SW off the main road past the Lahnersäge, the old water-powered sawmill. Keep on uphill and after crossing a bridge over a stream, fork L amid houses up the steep surfaced lane signed 'Zur Kirche' (to the church). Lined with modern-style stations of the cross, it quickly reaches the **Ultnerhof** guesthouse (1519m, 20min) and café close to the village's lovely white **church** with its landmark red steeple. Go R past Hotel Arnstein, and at the first curve in the road, branch L on the forestry lane. This proceeds NW on the edge of wood and emerald green pasture flats where well-fed cattle graze.

Ignore the fork L at a crucifix but a little further on, take the next R (n.140) across a bridge and splashing mountain stream **Falschauer**. Past a tiny abandoned mill is a traditional farm where you branch L. This leads through

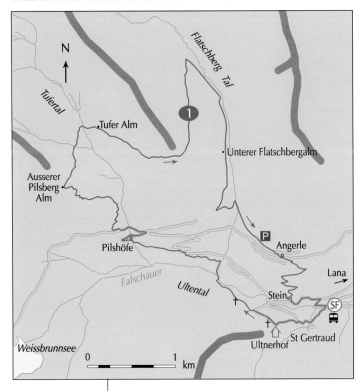

more farm premises on an old paved track that climbs steadily parallel to the road. As the tarmac is joined, go L for a matter of metres to where n.140 resumes as a lovely lane into woods, then a path climbing gently to meadows and across a stream into the timeless hamlet of **Pilshöfe** (1675m, 50min), home to reticent farming folk accustomed to living on near-vertical mountainsides. Fork R at the minor road and up to a four-way intersection. Now go L on n.142 (tarmac) for 5min to the signed turn-off where a clear path continues N. Through a wood of shady conifers, it climbs steadily, touching on a clearing and lopsided hut. Here the way bears WNW in tighter

zigzags, to emerge at the beautifully positioned **Ausserer Pilsberg Alm** (2128m, 1hr 30min), complete with a herd of goats, drinking fountain, an ancient crucifix and picnic benches with a gorgeous view of the upper valley and the Weissbrunnsee.

Strolling along the forestry lane after passing Hotel Arnstein

Suitably rested and refreshed, fork R (NNE) to a shoulder where you part ways with n.142 and keep N on n.12, a stroll through a carpet of juniper, alpenrose and bilberry shrubs. The glorious **Tufertal** soon reveals itself, a vast expanse of rolling pasture dotted with tiny shepherds' huts. Over the tinkling stream is photogenic **Tufer Alm** (2099m, 20min), with its sheep, pigs and jovial shepherd straight out of a 19th-century postcard.

Isolated **Alms**, tiny shepherds' huts fashioned out of ageing tree trunks and set in marvellous spots with vast alpine outlooks, stand hundreds of vertical metres over the Ultental valley floor and its pretty farming settlements. They occupy pasture either above the tree line or in clearings where rocks and plants have been painstakingly removed over time to give priority to the livestock such as sheep, goats

39

Beautiful Tufertal

and cows which are brought up here year in year out to feast on the fresh fragrant grass and alpine flowers all summer long.

Now n.12 returns to woodland on a roller-coaster traverse SE past Arolla pines with hosts of squawking nutcrackers and squirrels. At stock gates you head N to enter **Flatschberg Tal** (40min), where you turn R downhill on n.143, a lane parallel to a cascading torrent. Further on is the farm café-eatery **Unterer Flatschbergalm** (1905m), handy for a refreshment or meal stop. Soon afterwards the lane veers L to a **car park** then a surfaced road at **Angerle** (1783m) with plunging views to St Gertraud. Follow signs carefully to go R (SE) downhill and thread your way through old farm premises. Immediately after a modern crucifix keep your eyes peeled for red/white waymarks that point you L (SW at first) down on a woodland path that zigzags easily all the way down to the farms and houses of **Stein**. Here turn L along the road for the final 10min back to St Gertraud (1504m, 1hr 30min).

WALK 2
Höchsterhütte Circuit

Start/Finish	Weissbrunnsee car park
Distance	14km (8.7 miles)
Ascent/Descent	700m
Difficulty	Grade 2
Walking time	4hr 30min
Access	St Gertraud is the last stop on the year-round SAD bus run from Meran via Lana; a June–October shuttle bus (by Paris Ultental Reisen Tel 0473 791013) runs up the remaining narrow 6km as far as Weissbrunnsee/Lago Fontana Bianca. Otherwise drive up.

This is a long and immensely satisfying day walk that explores the uppermost Ultental. Beginning in dense conifer forest the route climbs to desolate slopes beneath a crown of pointed snowbound peaks and a remnant hanging glacier. It touches two photogenic lakes before embarking on a lovely descent through pasture terraces dotted with sheep and goats, and characteristic shepherds' huts.

A couple of hours from the start is Höchsterhütte/Rifugio Canziani where a delicious lunch can be enjoyed on the terrace overlooking Grünsee/Lago Verde. Otherwise go prepared (supplies can be purchased at St Gertraud) and enjoy a picnic – the choice of spots is vast and inspiring.

From the **Weissbrunnsee** car park (1879m), follow the signs for n.140 past the **Knödlmoidl** restaurant then the private cable car that supplies the upper hydro dam where you are headed. The well-trodden path begins its climb SW through light woods of larch and Arolla pine. This is a delightful stretch, alongside the streams flowing from the many lakes up-valley. Ignore the turn-off L for Fischersee and Walk 3 (where the return leg slots in) and keep on upwards towards rugged outcrops as the trees and vegetation thin. After a waterfall, the wall damming Grünsee is visible ahead, but it looks deceptively like a moraine ridge. Towering overhead is Hintere

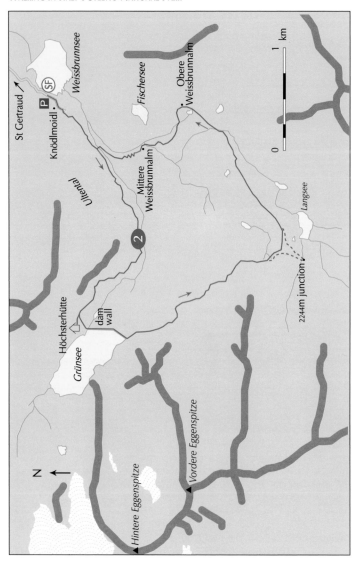

Eggenspitze/Cima Sternai, its glacier bed out of sight for the time being. ▶

A final steep stretch NW brings you out on a level with the dam, in a vast landscape of desolation and red rock where mere walkers are dwarfed. From here, it is not far to the scattering of modest Electricity Commission buildings, and welcoming **Höchsterhütte** (2560m, 2hr)

> **Höchsterhütte** has a grandiose setting on the edge of Grünsee which is fed by thundering cascades. The original 1909 German building is now at the bottom of the artificial lake. At the quiet, friendly substitute hut, excellent food such as the wholesome pasta dish *pizzoccheri* is served. It is a marvellous spot for drinking in the superb panorama, and this uppermost corner of Ultental is revealed as a magnificent amphitheatre with a crown of soaring peaks such as Hintere Eggenspitze west-southwest, identifiable by a cross on its summit.

Backtrack to where n.12 forks R (S) in descent to cross the **dam wall**. At the far end, the clear path wends

Underfoot are huge rock slabs, giant steps, flanked by spreads of bright alpenrose.

The steep climb towards the dam wall

43

its way around crumbly corners and in steady descent over enormous chunky slabs of red rock. It curves SSE with marvellous views over pasture and lakes below. At 2457m an especially scenic outcrop dotted with cairns marks the start of the drop towards stomach-shaped Langsee. A direct unnumbered path shortcuts SE down the grassy slope, but if you miss it (which is easy to do), just stay on n.12 – it meanders due S to pick up the main valley path n.107 at a **2244m junction**. Close at hand is lovely **Langsee/Lago Lungo** (2340m, 1hr 10min), which spreads over an elongated vale shaded by a multi-coloured earth ridge.

Turn L (NE) for the wide path through vast banks of alpenrose that brighten the slopes enjoyed by grazing cows and sheep. Never far from a chattering stream, proceed down a beautiful series of inter-connected flowered pasture terraces dotted with clumps of glacier-modelled roches moutonnées. A timber bridge leads to the clearing with shepherds' hut **Obere Weissbrunnalm** (2220m), before plunging in a L (W) curve down to the photogenic pasture basin run through with trickling alpine streams crossed on timber walkways. Keep over the rise on the

After Langsee it is a lovely downhill stroll

opposite side past the tiny **Mittere Weissbrunnalm** (2068m) and the junction with Walk 3 via Fischersee. You need path n.103, which acts as the link back down through the woods of larch and Arolla pine to rejoin path n.140 and turn R back to the Weissbrunnsee car park (1872m, 1hr 20min).

At Mittere Weissbrunnalm

> The name **roche moutonnée** makes for a curious tale. It would suggest their resemblance to recumbent sheep, but in fact the term was first coined by 18th-century Swiss explorer and pioneer mountaineer Horace-Bénédict de Saussure in a totally different vein. In his eyes the modelled rocks looked like the wigs in vogue at the time to which mutton fat (thus *moutonnée*) was applied to keep the hair in place!

WALK 3
Fischersee Walk

Start/Finish	Weissbrunnsee car park
Distance	6km (3.7 miles)
Ascent/Descent	200m
Difficulty	Grade 2
Walking time	2hr
Access	St Gertraud is the last stop on the year-round SAD bus run from Meran via Lana; thereafter a June–Oct shuttle bus (by Paris Ultental Reisen Tel 0473 791013) runs up the final narrow 6km as far as Weissbrunnsee. Otherwise drive this far.

A fascinating circuit high above Ultental and its thickly forested flanks, this walk guarantees superb views, a pretty lake, alpine meadows and carpets of glorious wildflowers. Meals and refreshments can be enjoyed at Fiechtalm, a dairy farm that doubles as a bustling alpine restaurant, otherwise Knödlmoidl at the very end of the walk.

The **Weissbrunnsee**, also called Lago Fontana Bianca, was dammed for hydroelectricity in the 1960s. According to legend, it was once the dwelling place of a voracious dragon who terrorised the local people. Fortunately, he was lured away by an enterprising visitor who harnessed him with red leather and rode the creature away downstream, never to be heard of again.

From the **Weissbrunnsee** car park (1879m), follow the signs for n.103 in common with n.140. Past the **Knödlmoidl** restaurant and cable car that supplies the upper hydro dam and its workers, the clear, well-trodden path begins its climb SW through light woods of mostly larch. Not far up you leave the route for Höchsterhütte (Walk 2) and fork L over a bridge and a pretty stream for a straightforward ascent S. The destination is the humble shepherd's abode **Mittere Weissbrunnalm** (2068m, 45min), which occupies

Old style dairy at Fiechtalm

a shoulder alongside a beautiful natural basin run through with meandering streams. Go L across the old timber bridge and briefly uphill over glacially polished rock slabs.

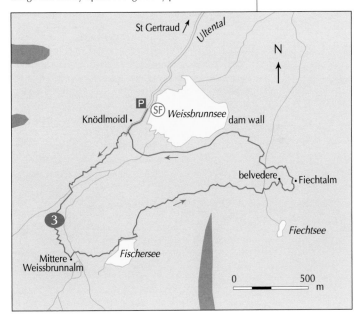

47

Lovely view over Weissbrunnsee

Beyond nestles pretty **Fischersee** (2068m), its water a blend of brilliant greens and blues.

At the path signposts at the far end, branch L past small-scale Electricity Board structures; ignore a turn-off for Weissbrunnsee and keep on n.107 as it narrows and makes its way NE through larch, pine and a dense carpet of bilberry shrubs and alpenrose. The next stretch is spectacular, running high above the Weissbrunnsee, crowned by conifers. It concludes at a **belvedere** outcrop. Now only a short descent away (R) is a dirt road and a busy alpine farm. Friendly **Fiechtalm** (2034m, 45min) serves meals and drinks to guests on a timber terrace, while its livestock are confined to age-old stalls if they are not enjoying the surrounding pasture.

Go L on signed path n.101 that makes its knee-testing way NE through woodland alive with squirrels. It finally concludes at a lane that runs L (W) past the **dam wall** at 1876m. Coasting around through low shrubby vegetation it swings past the southeast corner of the lake, to conclude at the car park at Weissbrunnsee (1879m, 30min).

WALK 4
Rifugio Lago Corvo

Start/Finish	Cavallar car park
Distance	11.5km (7.1 miles)
Ascent/Descent	1050m
Difficulty	Grade 2
Walking time	5hr 20min + 3hr extension
Access	Either drive up or catch a summer shuttle minibus – from San Bernardo and Rabbi Fonti (compulsory booking at Rabbi Fonti Visitor Centre). The run continues up the narrow farm track as far as Malga Caldesa Bassa, shortening the route if desired. The nearest bus stop is at Piazzola.

The walk is a long but straightforward ascent on farm lanes and paths through beautiful forest up to vast views. En route is Malga Caldesa Bassa, a working dairy-cum-eatery. Further uphill stands Rifugio Lago Corvo, another excellent place for a meal in the cosy wood-panelled dining room or al fresco. Do not get too weighed down, though, as a number of worthwhile sights are nearby.

First there is 2467m Passo di Rabbi, a short stroll away. This apparently insignificant saddle marks the passage between the Germanic province of Bozen in the north, and the predominantly Italian province of Trento to the south. But most visitors climb this far to admire the lakes, a bevy of jewels set in alpine cirques, wholly rock-locked. However, they are best admired from a higher vantage point, and a challenging extension for anyone with extra stamina and energy to burn is to the summit of Collecchio. A relentless 532m ascent, it guarantees amazing views of the lakes on a clear day, heaven for any photographer. An overnight stay at Rifugio Lago Corvo makes this extension more plausible.

Alternative access from Piazzola

Walkers with an interest in traditional alpine dwellings and barns will enjoy this. From the bus stop at **Piazzola** (1315m) walk E back along the road past the church where you need the signed path that cuts up L (due N) across fields and alongside a stream. On reaching a lane

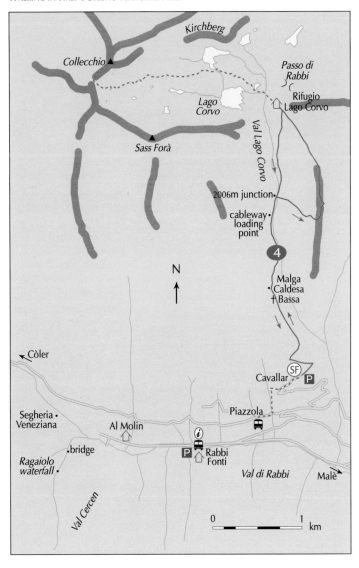

it turns R to the **Cavallar** car park where the walk begins (40min).

Traditional alpine dwellings at Piazzola

At the **Cavallar** car park (1420m) a signpost indicates a lane as n.108, through dense forest NE at first. Not far along is the first of two signed path shortcuts up L (NW). After those you veer R across a clearing with a picnic table, before embarking on a lovely woodland path WNW that verges on vertical in places. A tinkling alpine stream keeps you company on the last stretch before a farm lane is joined at a crucifix. Go R for the final metres to where the beautifully restored stone and timber buildings of alpine dairy farm **Malga Caldesa Bassa** (1835m, 1hr 10min) stand on the edge of thick forest. But do plod on as there is still a long climb to go.

Further along, keep your eyes peeled for the fork L where n.108 leaves the farm lane to resume its climb N across pasture run through with trickling water and thick with wildflowers. Another farm lane is crossed near the **cableway loading point** (1924m) for Rifugio Lago Corvo. Then it is not far uphill to a bridged stream crossing and **2006m junction** (50min), where the return route slots

51

The lakes are not far from the refuge

back in afterwards. A broad path, n.108 swings E then N in a wide curve, climbing quite steeply in parts, soon above the tree line and across bare terrain well grazed by sheep. After a fence barrier to prevent erosion by mountain bikes and a path junction (2372m), things level out, giving you time to appreciate the Sass Forà standing out W, and soon the hut ahead, sheltering in a protected saddle. Homely **Rifugio Lago Corvo** (2425m, 1hr) is also known as Rifugio Stella Alpina. The marvellous outlook takes in the Brenta Dolomites (southeast), the Tremenesca group (south) and the Presanella (southwest), as well as the Rabbi valley.

Once you can drag yourself away from the mouth-watering scents wafting out of the kitchen, keep walking to the lakes, scattered in photogenic rocky cirques. **Lago Corvo** is 10min away on path n.145, but a wander around the glacially smoothed boulders here reveals a clutch of lakes. ◂

Despite the name – 'corvo' means 'crow' – the tarns are home to the trout-like alpine charr, a rarity for this area.

Extension to Collecchio (3hr return)

Worth every minute of extra effort and drop of perspiration, path n.145 touches on a couple of lakes before

heading decidedly W for a faint path across broken rock rubble. Marker pillars of heaped-up stones point the steep way, which may include a snowfield in early summer. After a minor saddle comes the final leg to the cross on **Collecchio/Gleck** (2957m, 1hr 50min). The southernmost point of the Sternai chain, this is renowned as a breathtaking 360° lookout. ▸

Allow around 1hr 10min for the descent, and watch your step on the steep bits.

For the return route, immediately after the hut building an unmarked but clear path forks R off the main route to make its plunging way into **Val Lago Corvo**. It weaves S following the lines of the hut's supply cableway through rocky terrain interspersed with masses of wildflowers. It rejoins the main track down at the 2006m junction (40min).

From there, retrace the outward route to return via Malga Caldesa Bassa to the Cavallar car park (1420m, 1hr 40min).

The brilliant view from Collecchio down to the lakes and refuge

Apart from the occasional walker, tiny spiders and lichen apparently constitute the only other life forms here.

WALK 5
Rifugio Dorigoni Tour

Start/Finish	Còler car park
Distance	18km (11 miles)
Ascent/Descent	1200m
Difficulty	Grade 2
Walking time	6hr 30min
Access	Còler and its fee-paying car park are 3.5km from Piazzola by road. The nearest bus stop is at Plan (near Rabbi Fonti) – on foot allow 40min up the R bank of Torrente Rabbies. A summer shuttle bus runs from Còler (where tickets are sold) as far as Malga Stablasolo, saving 200m and 30min.

This popular walk passes close to the famous Cascate di Saent (visited in a more leisurely manner in Walk 7) before embarking on a long but memorable climb up terrace after terrace in beautiful, unspoilt Val di Saent. The day's destination is Rifugio Dorigoni, a comfortable alpine hut set in a vast cirque crowned by soaring summits and high-altitude snowfields. The return path is a little more demanding and less trodden. It loops through peaceful, little-visited La Valletta and follows a lofty path, before a knee-testing descent.

In all this makes for a lengthy and tiring day out with a hefty height gain and loss, so do start out early. Meals and snacks are available at Malga Stablasolo and Rifugio Dorigoni, while Stablet has a modest visitor centre with displays about marmots.

From the car park at **Còler** (1360m) head across the bridge then N past **Rifugio Al Fontanin** where the surfaced road gives way to a good lane. It is a short climb to the dairy farm **Malga Stablasolo** (1539m, 30min). Uphill on n.106 keep L at the intersection (ignore the fork R for the *cascate*), to the **Stablet Visitor Centre** (1589m). Here a path takes over, climbing easily through a veritable rock garden where masses of alpine pinks and mountain house leeks grow. Keep straight on through **Plan de le Scalace** (1640m) – where a detour is feasible to see the

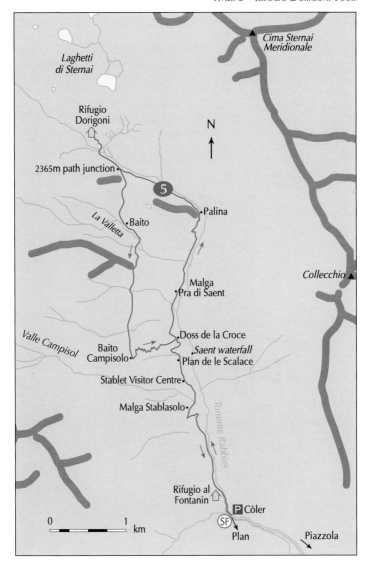

Laghetti di Sternai

Cima Sternai Meridionale

Rifugio Dorigoni

2365m path junction

N

5

La Valletta
•Baito

•Palina

Collecchio

Malga
•Pra di Saent

Valle Campisol

Baito
Campisolo•

•Doss de la Croce
Saent waterfall
•Plan de le Scalace

Stablet Visitor Centre•

Malga Stablasolo•

Torrente Rabbies

Rifugio al
Fontanin

P Còler
SF
Plan

Piazzola

0   1 km

marvellous Saent waterfalls – then up to a shoulder **Doss de la Croce** (1799m, 45min), a noted observation point for wildlife. This is where the return loop arrives later on.

The way now descends a little into the beautiful pasture valley of Pra di Saent lined with larches. Home to scampering marmots, the valley also has expanses of peat bog run through with streams. Towering above are the reddish flanks of the Sternai peaks. Further on are the modest timber buildings of **Malga Pra di Saent** (1784m, 15min), not far from another waterfall. ◄

Keep N past a picnic area on n.106 to embark on the *Sentiero degli Alpinisti* (mountaineers' path), a relentless

Here an optional 1hr 30min circuit breaks off to admire ancient larch trees.

On the 'Sentiero degli Alpinisti'

zigzagging sequence of flights of wooden steps with a guiding handrail cable on the steeper exposed bits. Needless to say, stops to catch your breath mean opportunities to enjoy wonderful views all around.

Looking up Val di Saent on the return path

> The variety of habitats in the unspoilt **Val di Saent** host a wealth of brilliant alpine plants and flowers, and chances are good of spotting roe and red deer, marmots and birds of prey. Patience and binoculars are recommended. In the mid-16th century the imperious Catholic Council of Trent banished witches to Pra di Saent.

A crest at 2100m (1hr) labelled **Palina** sees a move NW onto rather different terrain. Above the tree line now are found alpenrose, heather and bilberry shrubs in the company of black vanilla orchids, purple alpine asters and pink adenostyle. The climb assumes a much gentler gradient as it closely follows the bank of the gushing stream. Past the **2365m path junction** (for the return route), in sight of the refuge now, keep on across a marshy zone with plank bridges. Then it is only 100m up

57

to the ample natural platform and **Rifugio Silvio Dorigoni** (2437m, 1hr), named after a local dignitary and alpine club president. A well-deserved rest and picnic are in order as you admire Cima Rossa di Saent west, then Cima Mezzena and Cima Careser west-southwest.

Backtrack to the 2365m path junction (15min) and turn R on n.128. It traverses flowered grassland to a 2280m shoulder and picnic table with a extensive views. Now decidedly downhill, it enters **La Valletta**, a beautiful inner valley. After derelict hut **Baito** (2281m) it is down to a sturdy bridge, then R over a gushing torrent. Now narrower and rougher in spots with small ups and downs, the path leads over more streams and through bushes where chamois may be disturbed. It concludes with a final clamber up to beautifully situated **Baito Campisolo** (2126m, 1hr 15min), which has drinking water, benches, a toilet and gorgeous views over Val di Saent.

Grasp your trekking poles firmly and brace your knees for the abrupt path E through larch wood, down to Doss de la Croce (1790m, 30min).

Follow the ascent route in reverse back to Malga Stablasolo (1539m) then the car park at Còler (1360m, 1hr).

Laghetti di Sternai

A superb way to transform this walk into a two-day outing is to spend a night at Rifugio Dorigoni, to allow ample time for an extension following the 'Percorso naturalistico', a 2hr 30min circular nature trail marked with cairns. This entails a climb to see the seven pretty multi-coloured tarns, **Laghetti di Sternai**, dotted around a wild cirque at the foot of Cima di Rabbi. The highest of the tarns, Lago Nuovo (2862m), is relatively recent – it came into being 70 years ago following the retreat of the Vedretta di Rabbi hanging glacier. Refuge staff will provide a GPS and a guide.

WALK 6
Baito Campisolo Route

Start/Finish	Còler car park
Distance	11km (6.8 miles)
Ascent/Descent	800m
Difficulty	Grade 2
Walking time	5hr 15min
Access	Còler and its fee-paying car park are 3.5km from Piazzola by road in Val di Rabbi. The nearest bus stop is at Plan – on foot allow 40min up the R bank of Torrente Rabbies.

Compared to the Rifugio Dorigoni path (Walk 5), this marvellous high route is all but deserted, which increases chances of spotting animals – remember those binoculars. In fact this is one of the park's recognised trails, the 'Percorso della Fauna' (wildlife path). A steep slog through thick conifer forest leads up to panoramically placed alpine dairy farms strung along the western lip of Val di Saent. A prolonged traverse concludes with a narrow, moderately exposed stretch of path, on the approach to lookout par excellence Baito Campisolo. A knee-testing descent is followed by gentler gradients past the famous Saent waterfalls – visited in Walk 7.

Allow a full day for this outing and go equipped with plenty of food and drink – perfect picnic spots abound, some with drinking water. The only café-restaurant en route is Malga Stablasolo, on the last leg, although the Rifugio Al Fontanin guesthouse at the start and end of the walk also has pleasant al fresco facilities.

From **Còler** (1360m) follow the road across **Torrente Rabbies** and gently uphill to nearby **Rifugio Al Fontanin** (1443m, 5min). Soon after the building turn L on the path marked 'Percorso della Fauna'. Heading SW past old barns, it wastes no time climbing into cool conifer forest, quite steeply at times. A farm lane is joined in **Val Maleda** and the gradient eases considerably. It is a pleasant amble in the company of grazing cows up past summer farm **Malga Stablaz bassa** (1720m). ▸ Stick to the lane until you reach a signed shortcut that takes a faint

Opposite south are the soaring flanks of Monte Sole, while ahead Cima Verdignana and the lofty cirques close in the valley head.

59

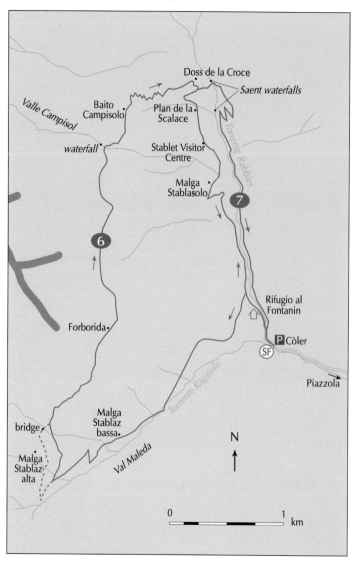

Doss de la Croce

Saent waterfalls

Baito
Campisol

Plan de la
Scalace

Valle Campisol

waterfall

Stablet Visitor
Centre

Malga
Stablasolo

Torrente Rabbies

7

6

Rifugio al
Fontanin

Forborida

Còler

SF

Piazzola

Torrente Ragaiolo

bridge

Malga
Stablaz
bassa

Malga
Stablaz
alta

Val Maleda

N

0   1
          km

mule track N out of the wood to the 2000m contour level near a bridge (2034m, 1hr 45min). (If you miss the turn-off never fear, as the lane continues in parallel, climbing towards Malga Stablaz alta. Where it veers L to the farm, you need to go R across the 2034m bridge to pick up the main route).

A broad track heads NNE on the edge of pasture and woodland. It is a pleasant jaunt to the information board and stone huts of **Forborida** (2124m, 30min) in a scenic position looking northeast across the Val di Saent to Collecchio as well as east down the valley to Rabbi and its hamlets. The path narrows a little, continuing essentially N along the middle section of Cima Ponte Vecchio, which remains out of sight, but the views all other directions are reward enough and it is worth making the most of the well-placed bench soon encountered. Ignore all the turn-offs, faint animal tracks for the most part. Two ample basin-like valleys separated by a modest outcrop are traversed in succession. On leaving the second, Pravedela (a reference to alpine pasture) the path drops down a shoulder. Watch your step on the slippery terrain as it leads into the

The waterfall crossing in Valle Campisol

*Beautifully positioned
Baito Campisolo*

narrow slit of **Valle Campisol** with its crashing **waterfall** and plank footbridge. Next a slender path cuts around a near-vertical mountainside with some exposure. It is only a short section, but a sure foot is needed. Not far around the corner on a natural platform stands the delightful hut **Baito Campisolo** (2126m, 1hr 15min).

After a suitable rest and due appreciation of the cool drinking water, civilised loo, not to mention wonderful views over verdant Val di Saent from the comfort of a bench, lengthen your trekking poles to help with the ensuing abrupt descent E through larch wood. This ends at the ample rock outcrop **Doss de la Croce** (1799m, 30min), another well-known spot for observing the deer and marmots that roam in the neighbouring Pra di Saent.

Fork R onto path n.106 in zigzagging descent to the clearing **Plan de le Scalace** (1640m), where a detour can be taken to visit the spectacular Saent waterfalls (see Walk 7). Keep on downhill alongside rock flanks bright with flowers to the **Stablet Visitor Centre** (1589m). Now a lane leads past the dairy farm and café-restaurant **Malga Stablasolo** (1539m), and downhill parallel to **Torrente Rabbies** back to Rifugio Al Fontanin (1443m) and Còler (1360m, 1hr 10min).

WALK 7
Cascate di Saent

Start/Finish	Còler car park
Distance	6km (3.7 miles)
Ascent/Descent	350m
Difficulty	Grade 1
Walking time	2hr 10min
Access	Còler and its fee-paying car park are 3.5km from Piazzola by road. The nearest bus stop is at Plan (upvalley from Rabbi Fonti) – on foot allow 40min up the right bank of Torrente Rabbies.
Note	See map on page 60

The undisputed highlight of this wonderful loop is the visit to the magnificent Cascate di Saent, the greatest waterfall in the Stelvio National Park. In Val di Saent in the upper Rabbi valley, the falls are fed by powerful Torrente Rabbies, which derives from surprisingly diminutive snowfields and remnant glaciers.

Apart from the initial section to Malga Stablasolo (which can be covered with a summer shuttle bus, saving 30min), the walk follows the 'Percorso geologico' (geological route) conceived by the park authorities to encourage visitors to take a closer look at the natural surroundings.

The outward section as far as the Plan de le Scalace picnic area is in common with Walk 5.

From the car park at **Còler** (1360m) head L across the bridge then N past café-restaurant **Rifugio Al Fontanin** where the surfaced road gives way to a good lane. From here it is a short climb to the dairy farm **Malga Stablasolo** (1539m, 30min), a rustic café-restaurant.

N.106 keeps on uphill. Just around the corner keep L at the intersection (ignore the fork R for the cascate) and you quickly reach the **Stablet Visitor Centre** (1589m) and its educational display about the life of marmots.

The path near the middle fall

Soon a path takes over, climbing easily through larch trees that filter the sunlight. On the adjacent rock faces masses of alpine pinks and mountain house leeks flourish. At the clearing and picnic area **Plan de le Scalace** (1700m, 40min), turn R to leave n.106. The well-trodden path leads downhill a little way crossing tree roots to the middle and most spectacular of the thundering falls. A timber bridge, soaked and slippery with clouds of flying spray, leads over the river, an exciting spot. ▶

The rock here – unlike the rest of the valley – is an especially durable granite that resists the force of the pounding water.

Most of the **rocks** in the valley are micaschists. They were originally fine-grained sedimentary material, such as sand or mud, that was subjected to heat and pressure, transforming it into metamorphic rocks. Fracturing and the effect of atmospheric factors, such as rain, continue to modify the landscape; a notable example was a landslide below the falls in September 1999, which caused widespread flood damage in the underlying valley.

A gentle descent on wood and paved steps through the trees leads to the lovely lower fall. Continue down to picnic tables (1549m), and ignore the fork R across the torrent (unless you hanker after the café facilities and shuttle bus of Malga Stablasolo). A clear path follows the bank of **Torrente Rabbies** to an information board then proceeds beneath steep grassy inclines dotted with trees, to lead easily alongside the watercourse and back to the car park at Còler (1360m, 1hr).

WALK 8

Ragaiolo Falls and the Venetian Sawmill

Start/Finish	Rabbi Fonti
Distance	4.5km (2.8 miles)
Ascent/Descent	230m
Difficulty	Grade 1–2
Walking time	1hr 30min
Access	Rabbi Fonti is served by year-round buses from Malè; car drivers will find ample parking near the spa and hotel.

This straightforward short walk is a perfect way to stretch your legs and start getting acquainted with this lovely valley. From the mouth of Val Cercen (explored fully in Walk 9), it is a short way uphill to visit a waterfall, followed by a stroll through woodland to a fascinating sawmill. Try and time your visit with a working demonstration – check with the Visitor Centre at Rabbi Fonti before setting out.

The closing leg of the walk passes the guesthouse-café Al Molin, should you be in need of refreshments.

From the bus stop and car park at **Rabbi Fonti** (1195m), walk W along the road for a matter of metres to where a good dirt road (n.109) branches L for Val Cercen and its dairy farms. This leads gently uphill WSW. After a little over 1km, fork R onto a marked path that cuts through woodland. This soon reaches picnic tables and a fenced-in **lookout** (1390m, 30min) onto the **Ragaiolo waterfall**, a single elegant stream of frothy water from a rock cleft chute.

Taking care on the slippery terrain, follow the flight of steps that zigzags down to the valley floor. At the lane turn L for the bridge across **Torrente Ragaiolo** to a signboard. Now branch R (NNW) on the path that leads through to the picnic area at the **Segheria Veneziana of Begoi** (1268m, 20min).

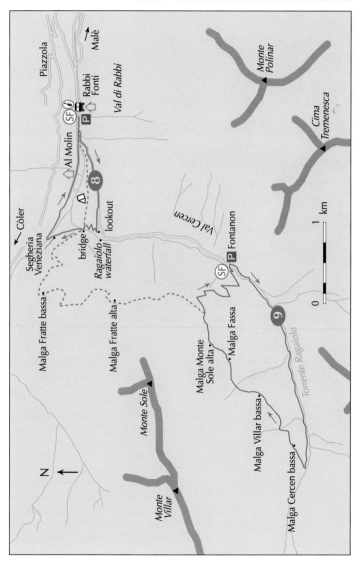

In the 13th century this type of **water-driven mill** was introduced across the Trentino and neighbouring alpine regions by the Republic of Venice. The *segherie* were crucial to satisfy its perpetual need for timber essential for the construction of the city and its ships. Ingenious constructions, the mills enabled a single man to cut hefty tree trunks into planks on his own.

The Segheria Veneziana of Begoi dates back to the 18th century. Thankfully the park authorities have seen fit to undertake full-scale maintenance and keep the mill up and

The Segheria Veneziana (Venetian sawmill)

running during the summer months, to the obvious delight of visitors, not to mention the skilled artisan responsible for the ancient mechanisms. Even if the mill is not in operation, there is still a lot to see and appreciate, starting at the rear of the building where the stream has been diverted into huge timber channels and chutes alongside the giant flapped wheel.

After a thorough visit, continue up the lane and keep R across Torrente Rabbies. An unsurfaced forestry lane leads SE parallel to the rushing stream, beneath towering conifers and a scattering of picturesque traditional timber chalets. Through the car park and past the turn-off for the camping ground, It is not far to **Al Molin café**, before the concluding stretch along the road back to Rabbi Fonti (1195m, 40min).

WALK 9
Val Cercen

Start/Finish	Fontanon car park, Val Cercen
Distance	10km (6.2 miles)
Ascent/Descent	500m
Difficulty	Grade 1–2
Walking time	3hr (4hr with Rabbi Fonti extension)
Access	Summer shuttle minibuses run up Val Cercen from San Bernardo and Rabbi Fonti to the Fontanon car park (compulsory booking at the Rabbi Fonti Visitor Centre). They occasionally continue up the narrow farm track as far as Malga Cercen bassa, a saving of 1hr 10min. Otherwise drive up to Fontanon, but be aware that the road is sometimes closed to private traffic.
Note	See map on page 67

This easy scenic circuit explores quiet Val Cercen, a branch of Val di Rabbi on the southernmost border of the Stelvio National Park. The route mostly follows wide farm lanes around the 2000m contour, touching on several interesting working dairy farms, which can be visited. The first, Malga Cercen bassa, boasts an impressive line-up of rounds of cheese, the production of a single season, and the staff willingly show visitors through the cool room. The second, Malga Monte Sole alta, has re-invented itself with great success as a gourmet, albeit rustic, eatery.

An extension described here leads to another great food venue, Malga Fratte bassa, and from there it is a simple matter to return to Rabbi Fonti on foot.

Leave the **Fontanon** car park (1549m) on the farm lane (n.109) that proceeds SW, soon crossing to the R bank of **Torrente Ragaiolo**. At the foot of the rock giants of the Tremenesca and Vegaia groups and patches of pasture carved out by man for grazing livestock, you ignore turn-offs and gently ascend Val Cercen. ▸ The lane curves up to **Malga Cercen bassa** (1969m, 1hr 10min). Rearing up southwest across the valley head is pyramidal Cima

Cows can be seen grazing on the verdant slopes, their neck bells jangling noisily.

Mouthwatering cheeses at Malga Cercen bassa

These open slopes are perfect for spotting birds of prey such as the golden eagle and the kestrel.

Grande, which will be a constant companion on the walk.

As signposted, keep R (ENE) here through light woodland and over a stream towards the next farm. At the long dark timber and stone cowsheds of **Malga Villar bassa** (2020m), you veer L almost immediately and leave the lane for a new faint path. Marked by low poles it strikes out NNE, climbing across pasture with bright patches of wildflowers. Another lane is joined for a leisurely traverse R (ENE) with magnificent views. From modest **Malga Fassa** (2057m) the view embraces the Tremenesca group to the south, while further west Cime Vallon and Grande close off the head of Val Cercen. ◄

Another short stroll will see you at **Malga Monte Sole alta** (2048m, 55min) complete with a playground and scenic picnic area looking east towards the mountains beyond Rabbi. As the name suggests, it is set on the southern flanks of modest Monte Sole.

Take the signposted path E that cuts the wide bends of the farm lane, heading in constant descent into lovely conifer woods. The second time the path intersects the lane, about 10min down, walkers on the extension to Rabbi need to keep L.

Extension to Rabbi Fonti (1hr 40min)
Stay on the lane in gentle descent NE to the next curve where a marked path breaks off N through the cover of beautiful larch and fir trees. The going is mostly level and leads to abandoned **Malga Fratte alta** (1867m), in a marvellously panoramic spot high over Rabbi Fonti and the valley. After the building, fork R downhill on the marked path that soon re-enters woodland on a knee-testing descent that concludes at lovely meadows surrounding **Malga Fratte bassa** (1482m, 1hr). With a backdrop of the Val di Saent, the lively farm-cum-eatery is usually a hive of activity, with picnickers galore and cows wandering in and out of the milking sheds. Turn R (SE) on the farm lane leading down to the **bridge** over Torrente Ragaiolo below the falls (see Walk 8). Here continue due E past the campsite and out to the road and from there to **Rabbi Fonti** (1195m, 40min).

Those aiming to complete the circuit walk will stay on the path, which soon has wide curves of its own. These finally end down on the valley floor and the bridge leading over Torrente Ragaiolo to the Fontanon car park (1549m, 55min).

Malga Monte Sole alta

WALK 10
Rifugio Larcher Tour

Start/Finish	Car park near Malga Mare
Distance	13.5km (8.4 miles)
Ascent/Descent	750m
Difficulty	Grade 2
Walking time	5hr + 2hr 20min extension
Access	At the termination of a narrowing mountain road 9km from Cogolo is the Malga Mare car park, fee-paying. No public buses reach this point (Cogolo is the nearest stop), but local taxis are always available to run walkers up and collect them afterwards.

This superb circuit with splendid scenery explores Val Venezia in the northern realms of Val di Peio. A range of glacial phenomena such as moraine ridges snaking down the valley edge below hanging glaciers, and excellent examples of roches moutonnées can be seen. Towering above are landmark peaks like the twin-peaked Cevedale and magnificent Palon de la Mare. The circuit is well within the reach of family groups and has plenty of interest with the string of lakes and wildlife. En route is beautifully located Rifugio Larcher al Cevedale, which makes an excellent destination in itself. Perched on an outcrop directly opposite an ice spill, the place hums with activity throughout the summer months.

A recommended if more difficult side trip is also to La Forcola, a 3032m vantage point that opens onto a breathtaking icescape as you peek over a glacier spread into Martelltal. Even in midsummer, the final stretch may be tricky and icy, so check with the staff at Rifugio Larcher before proceeding.

From the **Malga Mare** car park (1972m) alongside the old-style electricity commission buildings and small reservoir, take popular path n.102 due N past a snack bar and quickly uphill to the elongated cowshed, now beautifully renovated as cosy alpine eatery Malga Mare (2031m). Then it is N uphill in wide curves with colourful masses of alpenrose beneath the occasional larch and Arolla pine. The steady climb leads through a series of picturesque level natural terraces run through with meandering streams, their banks colonised by fluffy white cotton grass and fat yellow globeflowers. In the meantime, west-southwest the sprawling glacier Vedretta Rossa comes into view on Monte Vioz, and not long after you can even admire the Cevedale. At 2290m the path enters immense **Pian Venezia** (1hr), with a park hut and path junction (where a shortcut to Lago Lungo is feasible).

A gentle climb NNW remains, up the right-hand side of **Val Venezia**, the panorama widening at every step. Rifugio Larcher is already visible ahead, although your eyes will probably be fixed on the great moraine walls west across the valley beneath the ice and snow cascade of multi-crevassed Vedretta de la Mare. Once you get to **Rifugio Larcher** (2608m, 1hr) it is even more spectacular. Dramatic colour tone contrasts are provided by the khaki-brown moraine, lichen-stained green rock, red scree, blue ice and white snow. Settle down to savour the sights with a lunch of hearty barley soup (*zuppa d'orzo*) and a slice of home-made cake.

Approaching Rifugio Larcher

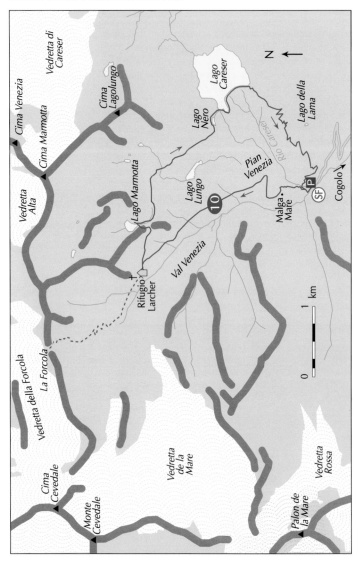

Extension to La Forcola (2hr 20min return)

▸ In front of the refuge's dining room door, take path n.103 NW. Passing close to a tiny **chapel**, it dips into the valley floor to begin ascending in earnest on a narrowing but clear path, possibly in the company of dainty chamois. Once over a ridge about 45min up, you lose sight of the refuge and soon engage in a sequence of tight zigzags. All effort is amply repaid as you reach breathtaking **La Forcola/Fürkelescharte** (3032m, 1hr 20min). As well as finding yourself on the border between Italian-speaking Trentino and German-speaking Südtirol, you are directly above vast glaciers, a gently rolling frozen sea of ice and snow, sloping down to the huts in Martelltal. Mountain-wise, northwest are the magnificent Gran Zebrù and Ortler, close-by west is towering Cevedale, while back southeast the elegant Brenta Dolomites stand out.

Return with care the same way to Rifugio Larcher (2608m, 1hr).

From the refuge take well-trodden path n.104 due E. It climbs easily to a 2726m ridge where you detour L (N) across to lovely **Lago Marmotta** (2704m, 30min). The banks are thick with cotton grass and summer picnickers, whose presence sets off the sentinels of the

Expect snow and ice on the final approach and be prepared to turn back if conditions are unfavourable.

At Lago Marmotta

resident marmots whose cries echo around this side valley. However, the ravenous flocks of alpine choughs are not deterred and the occasional eagle may also be spotted.

Leave the lake along the stream that drains it, to rejoin the main path n.104. Near small-scale sluice gates ignore the variant R via Lago Lungo and keep on the level path which bears R (SSE). Keep R on n.123 (n.104 climbs away NE to traverse the Vedretta di Careser), which soon makes a short detour to avoid a tunnel. It coasts in the company of spreads of bright wildflowers – spotted gentians and round-headed rampions stand out – while across Val Venezia is the fantastic panorama stretching from Monte Vioz to Palon de la Mare. ◄

> Despite its affinity to the Italian word *mare* for 'sea', this toponym derives from the pre-Roman term *lamara* denoting a heap of stones.

Past the shores of pretty **Lago Nero** (2624m) is the vast milky turquoise expanse of **Lago Careser** (2603m, 1hr), where huge black glacier-polished rocks lie recumbent like beached whales. Follow the dam wall (open to walkers from late June to late September – at other times you need to take the steep down-and-up detour path that rejoins the main route at the far end of the dam wall). At the Electricity Commission custodian's quarters at the far end, a rest stop will give you time to take stock of the gorgeous line-up of peaks, before you return to the valley floor.

> The abundance of **flowing water** from the melting ice masses has been put to good use by the Italian Electricity Board with a dam at Lago Careser connected via Malga Mare to the power station lower down near Cogolo. The remainder belongs to the Torrente Noce Bianco which joins the main river in Val di Sole.

The pleasant descent path heads SW in constant wide zigzags beneath the ridge of Le Lame, and affords views down Val di Peio to the flat-topped Presanella-Vermiglio in the background south-southwest, as well as delightful Lago della Lama close at hand. It moves into the cover of woods once more, and swings W before touching on the grazing flats preceding the Malga Mare car park (1972m, 1hr 30min).

WALK 11
Monte Vioz

Start/Finish	Rifugio Doss dei Cembri
Distance	14.5km (9 miles)
Ascent/Descent	1330m
Difficulty	Grade 3
Walking time	6hr 30min + 30min for the lifts
Access	From Peio Fonti (1383m), a cable car runs up to Rifugio Scoiattolo (1998m), from where a chairlift proceeds to Rifugio Doss dei Cembri (2315m).

Despite the breathtaking (literally!) height gain of 1330m, the walk up Monte Vioz at 3645m is a huge treat for walkers. Glacier-free, it is immensely popular in midsummer, boasting spectacular summit views. The way up is pleasant too, as Monte Vioz stands isolated from neighbouring ridges, on the southern edge of the Ortler group, and is an excellent all-rounder.

The route is rated 'sentiero alpinistico', which means a path with some exposure, a little difficulty and high altitude; notwithstanding this it is well within the reach of fit walkers as far as Rifugio Mantova al Vioz (5hr 50min round trip). The section to the summit is reserved for those who have a clear head for heights and a sure tread. However, overall good conditions are imperative, including absence of snow on the final summit stretch (unless you possess crampons, ice pick and experience). In adverse weather it can be exposed to bitter winds and there is no shelter before the rifugio. Moreover even when hot weather in the valleys dictates shorts and T-shirts, walkers must carry warm windproof clothing as well as sun protection, energy foods and plenty of water for the strenuous ascent. August–September is generally the best time to go, but conditions vary from year to year. Check locally before setting out. It is imperative to start out early and take note of the lift operating schedules to avoid missing the last run down!

From **Rifugio Doss dei Cembri** (2315m) take the dirt track a short way up Val della Mite to where the well-signed path n.139 for Rifugio Mantova al Vioz breaks off R (N). The few larch trees and even grass are quickly left behind and it is soon all scree and stark rock. Climb steadily

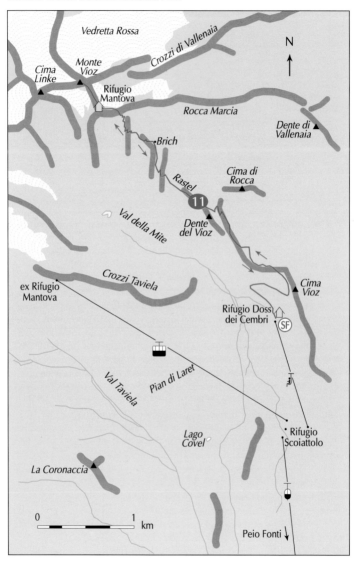

to a broad ridge to fork L (NW) on path n.105. Not far along is modest **Cima Vioz** scattered with WWI remains. Constantly NW, the path hugs an elongated ridge, offering vast views alternating on both sides. Several narrow tracts with marginal exposure are encountered, where extra care is needed. After rounding the base of the sharp bread-knife **Dente del Vioz** comes a stretch known as the **Rastel**, then the way becomes steeper but well graded. Stops for getting your breath back and acclimatising provide the chance to drink in the ever-expanding panorama, including the glittering Lago del Careser beneath its flat glacier hemmed in by impressive peaks.

It's a long climb up!

The **Brich** (3206m) means a short aided section across unstable terrain, after which the path heads up a near-vertical mountain flank, zigzags taking the sting out of the ascent. In due course you climb out at the tiny chapel and **Rifugio Mantova al Vioz** (3535m, 3hr 30min), located on the southern shoulder of Monte Vioz, overlooking icy Vedretta di Vioz.

For walkers with energy left to burn, the summit awaits. Take the clear if rocky path up the exposed and narrow ridge running NNW between two sheer ice and

At Rifugio Mantova, the highest manned hut in the Central Alps

snow-bound slopes. Soon after reaching a large cross is the summit itself, on more level ground and marked by a trig point. This is **Monte Vioz** (3645m, 20min).

> Monte Vioz is reportedly named after a **horse**. Vioz was a trusty steed on a desperate journey with his heroic master Adalbert, a young German prince who perished on the summit in mysterious circumstances. The sprawling glacier on the mountain's northeastern flanks is the Vedretta Rossa, 'red glacier', so named when the ice was tinged by the tears of blood wept by Adalbert's mother on learning of her son's death.

The breathtaking sights need time to sink in as 13 peaks surround the magnificent Forni glacier at your feet. From the north, moving anticlockwise, the principal mountains are Cevedale, Palon de la Mare, far-off Königspitze north-northwest, Pizzo Tresero west-southwest and Punta San Matteo southwest. To the south on a good day Adamello and the Presanella are visible. **Take great care not to inadvertently move onto dangerous snow cornices.** ◄

Incredibly, an Austrian front ran along these arduous crests during WWI, and tangled barbed wire still litters the slopes.

A wonderful way to experience the Vioz peak and make the trip more relaxing, is to stay overnight at the **Rifugio Mantova al Vioz** then enjoy a legendary sunrise. At 3535m this modern building with state-of-the-art technology is the highest manned hut in the whole of the Central Alps. Its predecessor was inaugurated just over 100 years ago in 1911, courtesy of the German-Austrian Alpine Club. It functioned as an army garrison during WWI, supporting a summit position. After the war the building was transferred to SAT, the Trentino Alpine Club.

An even earlier 1908 hut (ex-Rifugio Mantova) stood on the adjoining jagged crest Crozzi Taviela, where the ultra modern cable car Peio 3000 pulls in today. The cable car is controversial to say the least: since it began operation in 2011 brand new ski pistes and service trails have been gashed out – all inexplicably within the realms of the national park.

Return the way you came to Rifugio Mantova (3535m, 20min). Afterwards, retrace your steps on path n.105 all the way down to Rifugio Doss dei Cembri (2315m, 2hr 20min) to ride the lifts back to Peio Fonti.

Breathtaking Monte Vioz

WALK 12

Sentiero dei Tedeschi

Start	Rifugio Doss dei Cembri
Finish	Peio Fonti
Distance	16.5km (10.3 miles)
Ascent	365m
Descent	1275m
Difficulty	Grade 2–3
Walking time	5hr + 30min for the lifts
Access	From Peio Fonti (1383m) a cable car runs up to Rifugio Scoiattolo (1998m), from where a chairlift proceeds to Rifugio Doss dei Cembri (2315m).

Beginning with an effort-free panoramic ride on two linked lifts, this hugely rewarding traverse high along the western branch of Val di Peio offers solitude, vast views, spreads of lovely wildflowers and an abundance of wildlife. It is a long day out – necessitating an early start – and there is no shelter en route, so do wait for a clear day with settled weather. The only 'emergency exit' is at the Colen saddle, not far in. Copious drinking water and food supplies should be carried, along with sun protection as most of the day is spent above the tree line. There are a couple of narrow moderately exposed sections, which make it unsuitable for beginners.

This route is known as 'Sentiero dei Tedeschi' (path of the Germans) because it follows a route mapped out by German and Austrian troops during WWI. It touches on a string of wartime positions that involved Valle degli Orsi and Punta San Matteo high above. Immediately afterwards the path plunges valleywards into welcome tree cover, to follow an old military road that takes wide curves down to Malga Termenago di Sotto. Here a summer shuttle bus can be flagged down as an alternative to the final 20min along the road, bringing the huge circuit to its close at Peio Fonti.

From **Rifugio Doss dei Cembri** (2315m) take the dirt track (n.138) NW for a short distance uphill in Val della Mite to pick up n.139. This points you away from the crowds, L across a stream then over a new ski piste SW. The majority of walkers – most of them heading for Monte Vioz

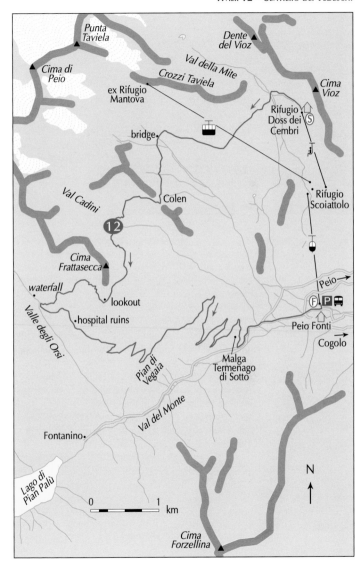

The chairlift to Rifugio Doss dei Cembri

– are quickly left behind as you move SW mostly on a level gradient across dry, sun-blessed terrain that is thick with heather, bell flowers and gentians. Soon overhead are the cables and cabins of the ultra-modern Peio 3000 cable car on their way up to the Crozzi Taviela ridge. As far as the marvellous views go, ahead southwest is Punta di Ercavallo, with dark crests swinging around via Punta d'Albiolo towards the south to connect with Monte Redival, whereas southeast the pale Brenta Dolomites stand out in the distance.

Once you reach inner Val Taviela below Punta Taviela, a cascading stream is crossed on a swaying **suspension bridge**. The path then bears S, aided by short stretches of fixed cable across rock surface. A brief unstable, crumbly passage requires a little extra care prior to the grassy saddle **Colen** (2368m, 1hr 20min).

The rocky ground here is home to twittering ground-nesting birds, while sheep and goats appreciate the pasture which spills downhill.

At the path junction here – unless you need the exit route to Peio here on n.129 (allow at least 1hr 30min) – keep R on the upper path branch, to climb gently into beautiful **Val Cadini** dominated by moraine crests. ◀ Further on comes a **lookout** (2532m, 1hr) beneath Cima Frattasecca. Here old stone walls from military installations afford fine views onto Lago di Pian Palù with its turquoise hues.

Punta San Matteo, northwest of Cima Frattasecca, is the site of what was (until the Kargil War of 1999) the highest battle in history, when Italian and Austro-Hungarian forces clashed on 3 September 1918 during WWI. The peak gained its name in 1867 when leading mountaineer Julius Payer scaled it on 21 September, St Matthews' Day. During the war the construction of fortifications together with the ruinous effect of bombardments lowered the top by a good 6m – its current height is 3678m.

The suspension bridge in Val Taviela

A lovely curving path drops across a boulder field of stepped rock slabs. At a path junction, leave n.139 (for Bivacco Meneghello) and branch L downhill on n.122A over grassy hillocks to a path junction near the lively waterfall that gushes through a deep rock cleft in **Valle degli Orsi** (2480m, 30min).

> **Valle degli Orsi** translates as 'valley of the bears'. Nowadays this beautiful, peaceful spot is ideal for picnics, with carpets of flowers. However, during WWI the valley acted as an essential supply channel for the Austrian strongholds on Punta San Matteo northwest and the crests adjoining eastwards.

Turn sharp L (SE) on n.122 cutting down heather slopes. At 2349m are wartime **hospital ruins** in the cover of shady woodland. Further on, stick to n.122 which will entail branching L (SE) at a path junction (ignoring n.129 which heads SW towards Lago Pian Palù). It drops past conifers and carline thistles to join a more relaxing jeep-width track that is an old military road (n.124) at **Pian di Vegaia** (1940m, 50min).

Go L – in common with Walks 13 and 14 – and enjoy views through the forest and the wide bends; ignore all turn-offs as you make your leisurely way down to the picnic area at **Malga Termenago di sotto** (1523m, 1hr), also known as Malga Frattasecca di sotto. Here you may strike lucky and be able to pick up the summer shuttle bus back to Peio Fonti, otherwise go L to walk back along the surfaced road to **Peio Fonti** (1383m, 20min).

WALK 13
Malga Covel and Waterfalls

Start/Finish	Cable car parking area at Peio Fonti
Distance	14km (8.7 miles)
Ascent/Descent	700m
Difficulty	Grade 1–2
Walking time	3hr 20min
Access	Peio Fonti is easily reached by car or bus; the car park is in Via del Fontanino, encountered as you enter the village, and the bus stops opposite.

This quiet, medium-altitude circuit along northern Val del Monte (off Val di Peio) wanders through a pretty alpine village and dairy farming hamlets, touching on a batch of modest waterfalls. An interesting detour takes in San Rocco, a poignant cemetery for victims of the Great War who perished in the vicinity. The majority of the graves were shifted to Rovereto in 1921, however remains of soldiers recovered as recently as 2009 from Punta San Matteo (see Walk 12) have been laid to rest here.

By all means catch the bus to Peio Paese (the village) and save yourself half an hour and 200m in ascent (from the village bus terminal walk W through to the church to pick up the route). But be aware this will mean missing an added attraction close to the start: the area faunistica for injured wildlife. The walk follows straightforward lanes and clear paths, although one short steep stretch between Malga Covel and Cascata Cadini necessitates a little extra care.

From the car park for the cable car at **Peio Fonti** (1383m) turn E along Via dei Cavai past Hotel Sporting and very soon L on the well-signed fork for the **area faunistica**. After crossing the meadow, keep uphill and take the path flanking the topmost enclosures. A short stretch of lane leads to the road which you follow for a matter of metres uphill R. Not far along, at some new houses, cross over to take a narrow road lined with lamp posts. A pedestrian way, it climbs gently staying above the traffic. As it enters the settlement, keep L (W) uphill on Via San Giorgio past

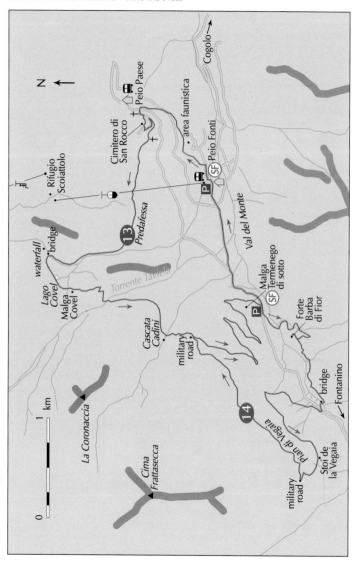

old houses. This emerges at a car park in the main square of **Peio Paese** (1579m, 30min), dominated by a 15th-century church and bell tower frescoed with a massive St Christopher figure standing 7m tall.

The village of Peio Paese

Nearby is a large path signboard where you branch L along the narrow surfaced road Salita di San Rocco past the hotel of the same name. Immediately after a shrine fork R on the clear path that climbs the wooded outcrop to the **Cimitero di San Rocco** and 15th-century chapel of the same name, marked by a dramatic slender pyramidal memorial. After a wander around the park, take the lane leading out the other side for the tarmac and go L downhill to regain the road where you turn R (W). The detour to San Rocco can be omitted if preferred by staying on the road at the shrine – saving 20min.

Past a crucifix and bench with a lovely view along Val del Monte below, a lane (n.125) leads under the cable car and past picturesque clusters of old farmhouses set amid the well-groomed meadows of **Predafessa**. A path through woods joins a minor road at a car park near old low-roofed houses. At the nearby path junction leave n.125 (it veers L) for the unnumbered path that continues due N on the R bank of a stream. Passing a dark timber hut and through trees, it soon hugs the edge of meadows. Past giant boulders used for rock climbing practice, the way soon reaches a pretty waterfall and a small **bridge**. Keep on L (W) past shallow marshy **Lago Covel** on the lower edge of larch forest. ◄

This is home to a thriving colony of minnows, reportedly a rare alpine species.

It is not far to **Malga Covel** (1856m, 1hr), a summer dairy farm that sells home-made cheeses. Walk past the picnic area and down the lane to a group of huts, where you need the next fork R (n.125). Initially a steep descent, it dips across the eroding margin of the valley sculpted by Torrente Taviela – watch your step. It quickly becomes a lovely path climbing SSW through silent conifer woods. Gushing **Cascata Cadini** (1800m) can be admired from a walkway. Not far along you join an old **military road** at 1794m, following its generous curves in leisurely descent. On the valley floor is a picnic area at **Malga Termenago di sotto**, also known as Malga Frattasecca di sotto (1523m, 1hr 30min). Here you may strike lucky and be able to pick up the summer shuttle bus back to Peio Fonti, otherwise go L to walk back along the surfaced road to the start (1383m, 20min).

Old farm en route to Lago Covel

90

WALK 14
Forte Barba di Fior Loop

Start/Finish	Malga Termenago di sotto
Distance	11km (6.8 miles)
Ascent/Descent	500m
Difficulty	Grade 2
Walking time	3hr 20min
Access	From Peio Fonti either take the summertime shuttle bus for Fontanino and alight at Malga Termenago di sotto (also known as Malga Frattesecca) or drive – if the road is open to the public. If starting out on foot from Peio Fonti allow an extra 40min return.
Note	See map on page 88

This circular route was put together by the park authorities to link up a scattering of minor historic sites which testify to WWI. En route are information boards with maps. Located close to the former Italian border, Val del Monte was relentlessly contested by both armies during the war, and traces of occupation can still be seen at all altitudes.

Photogenic albeit ruined Forte Barba di Fior is the star of the walk and makes a worthwhile outing in itself. Perched on a strategic outcrop, it looks forlornly down to Peio Fonti and across the neighbouring mountains from what is now a thickly wooded vantage point. A jaunt alongside an attractive mountain stream follows, then you cross the road for a steep ascent through woodland and a long traverse to visit a web of old tunnels used as shelter and storage for ammunition – a torch comes in handy here. The return stretch uses a pleasant panoramic lane, which is a former military road that returns to valley level in a series of vast wide curves.

On the opposite side of the road from **Malga Termenago di sotto** (1523m), take the signed lane (n.110) SW to descend to the bridge across Torrente Noce. The ensuing climb, paved in parts, winds through flowered meadows and past a cliff that guides use to teach rock climbing to beginners. Up on the ridge, keep R at the junction for **Forte Barba di Fior** (1610m, 25min), an atmospheric spot with extensive

Bright lichen near Forte Barba di Fior

It is worth taking time to explore the crumbling tunnels that served the army as shelters and storage.

views east. Backtrack briefly to the junction and now keep R (SW) for the narrowing path that drops through tree cover towards the level of the stream. A batch of boulders bright with yellow lichen stands out on the way to the fork R off n.110 (which continues WSW for Fontanino di Celentino) to a **bridge** (1580m).

You soon arrive back at the road (20min) at a mapboard and the start of a new path. This rises through conifer forest ENE very steeply at times. Once out of the trees, it goes through an open marshy area colonised with green alders to climb up to a path fork (1761m, 40min). Unless you prefer to shortcut, ignore the branch R (which quickly leads to the military road) and instead turn sharp L (SW again) mostly on a level. This rather lengthy traverse heads through woodland, narrow at times, and climbs every now and again. It finally reaches **Stoi de la Vegaia** (1900m, 30min), a clearing in the woods. ◄

On the next stretch both the path and waymarking are a little sketchy, but essentially you go NW with a few zigzags in ascent to join the broad and relaxing jeep-width track (n.124) which is an old **military road** (10min). Turn R here to **Pian di Vegaia** (1940m) where faint traces remain of wartime trench lines. There are also welcoming picnic tables and an information board, not to mention lovely views to be enjoyed. Ignore all turn-offs as you make your leisurely way down the wide curves to finally reach the picnic area at Malga Termenago di sotto (1523m, 1hr 15min).

WALK 15
Lago di Pian Palù Circuit

Start/Finish	Fontanino di Celentino
Distance	10km (6.2 miles)
Ascent/Descent	440m
Difficulty	Grade 1
Walking time	3hr 15min
Access	Fontanino di Celentino is located in Val del Monte 4.5km from Peio Fonti. It can be reached on the summer shuttle bus from Peio Fonti or by car when the road is open.

Passing through woodland and open pasture, this delightful walk circles a lovely lake. It passes sites where charcoal burning was practised in the 15–16th centuries and again in the mid-1800s, to supply the furnaces for the Val di Peio iron foundries. It is a good first walk as it is straightforward and is suitable for families. Clear tracks and paths are followed, and upper Val del Monte at the halfway mark is a good spot for observing wildlife.

True to its name, **Fontanino** is the location of an renowned source of natural mineral water. Ferruginous and rich in carbon dioxide, its medicinal properties run from laxative and diuretic to being beneficial to the liver, kidneys and the nervous system. Over-indulgence is inadvisable. Alongside is a summer restaurant and picnic area.

At **Fontanino** (1680m), just downhill of the thermal spring shelter, fork uphill (NE) on the forestry lane n.110B. This climbs decisively to a hairpin bend (SW) through a side valley colonised by green alder that flourishes in the boggy terrain. A steep stretch gains the level of the dam wall and the lake's edge (1800m). Here, ignoring a lower route, it climbs further as n.124B through pasture clearings enjoyed by grazing cows, to the path junction close to **Malga Giumella** (1930m). Now make an abrupt turn L (SW) on the mostly level

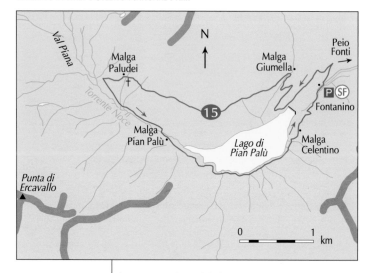

lane (n.124) through light woods of larch and pine trees where charcoal burners once worked. Ignoring turn-offs, after a wooden bridge and boggy terrain, you emerge on open grassland near a crucifix at **Malga Paludei** (2128m, 1hr 30min), on the southern edge of the magnificent Val Piana. Opposite, waterfalls cascade down the terraced flanks beneath Corno dei Tre Signori (due west) and Punta di Ercavallo (southwest), while the slopes above are home to herds of chamois who keep their distance from livestock.

Duly rested, point your boots valleywards on path n.110, which curves SE past a cluster of ancient larch trees to follow gushing **Torrente Noce** down its L bank. Within sight of the lovely lake, ignore the path branch n.110B (that hugs the L bank), and fork R across a timber bridge to **Malga Pian Palù** (1850m) and a refreshing drinking fountain and picnic bench. Heading into the cover of conifer woods, the wide track climbs briefly over a modest rise to lead mostly E. It stays well above the water level at first, affording continuous enjoyable vistas of the lake's multi-coloured surface. Passing

Lago di Pian Palù and its dam

semi-submerged boulders, it goes through a short tunnel near the far end and the dam – take care not to miss the fork R (NE) as n.110 heads across the meadows around **Malga Celentino** (1830m). Now a long ramp-like track leads rapidly downhill well beneath the dam wall back to Fontanino (1680m, 1hr 45min).

> **Lago di Pian Palù** was blocked off in the 1950s for hydroelectric purposes, and has a capacity of 13 million cubic metres; however, the 52m high dam itself has a low visual impact and hardly affects this beautiful spot, which is popular with picnicking families throughout summer. The lake water is remarkably varied in colour, beginning the day as a transparent deep alpine blue that morphs into bright turquoise around mid-afternoon as the melt water from snowfields and glaciers flows in, bearing suspended powdered rock that makes it opaque until it has time to drop to the bottom.

Lago di Pian Palù can also be brilliant turquoise

WALK 16

Dosso Tresero

Start/Finish	Piazza Magliavaca, Santa Caterina Valfurva
Distance	10.5km (6.5 miles)
Ascent/Descent	650m
Difficulty	Grade 1–2
Walking time	3hr 40min
Access	Santa Caterina Valfurva can be reached by Perego bus from Bormio; the stop is outside the tourist office in Piazza Magliavaca. It is possible to drive as far as La Centrale, a saving of 40min.

A delightful and easy walk that climbs through woodland to Dosso Tresero, a grassy belvedere platform with fine views on the middle section of immense Pizzo Tresero, which looms over the basin of Santa Caterina Valfurva. Good clear paths are followed, making it suitable for all walkers. Nearby is Pian delle Marmotte, and sightings of these delightful animals are not difficult. You may also see chamois.

From Piazza Magliavaca at **Santa Caterina Valfurva** (1740m) cross the covered timber bridge over Torrente

Piazza Magliavaca

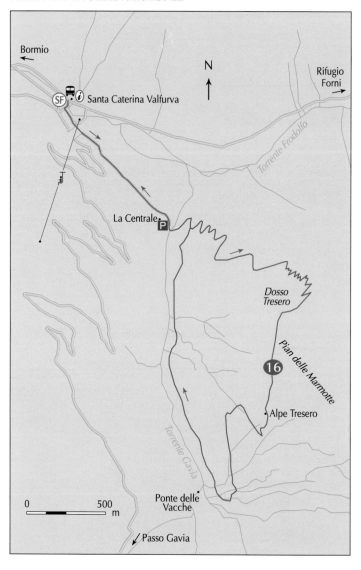

On Dosso Tresero

Frodolfo and turn L (SW) along the road lined with shops and through the tunnel under a chairlift. Past a handful of hotels and meadows it reaches an old power station building, **La Centrale** (1752m, 20min), with mapboards and a picnic area. Follow signs across a bridge over **Torrente Gavia**, keeping to forks for Dosso Tresero and the route referred to as 'La Romantica' (n.561). This quickly becomes a lovely zigzagging path still SW, climbing into mixed conifer woods, offering ever-improving views. As the trees thin, alpenrose and blueberry shrubs take over for the final climb to **Dosso Tresero** (2356m, 1hr 45min), far below Pizzo Tresero. Out with that compass: east-northeast rises the twin-pointed Cevedale, while Corno Tre Signori rises south over Passo Gavia.

Take the faint path (n.561) S in gentle descent across grassed slopes following low poles with red/white paint stripes, past a repeater. From here it is not far to the long-abandoned buildings of **Alpe Tresero** (2266m), in a sea of soft-topped grass and purple monk's-hood flowers and huge rock slabs. An old farm track leads downhill into woodlands dominated by Arolla pine and noisy nutcrackers. As it approaches the valley floor and stream, with Ponte delle Vacche, make sure you do not miss the fork R (NNW) for pretty path n.558. This runs high above Torrente Gavia across a number of marshy patches, rock slabs and tree roots. At a wide forestry track branch R and you soon curve down to the bridge at La Centrale (1752m, 1hr 15min) once more. Return along the road to Santa Caterina (1740m, 20min).

WALK 17

The Forni Sentiero Glaciologico Alto

Start/Finish	Rifugio Forni
Distance	9km (5.6 miles)
Ascent/Descent	600m
Difficulty	Grade 1–2
Walking time	3hr 20min
Access	From Santa Caterina Valfurva a narrow 5.5km road climbs to Rifugio Forni and car parks. A jeep taxi service is also available.
Note	At the time of writing this newly created route was not shown on any of the walking maps

This is a warmly recommended straightforward walk with plenty of interest and spectacular views of the Ghiacciaio dei Forni, Italy's most extensive valley glacier. Despite the walk title, no glacier crossings are involved, although the route does take you close to the glacier mouth, and past moraine ridges, vast rock slabs and surfaces polished and grooved by the passage of the ice. Rifugio Albergo Ghiacciaio dei Forni (usually shortened to Rifugio Forni) is a hospitable establishment dating back to 1896.

Two small Himalayan-style bridges (Ponti Tibetani) cross the two main meltwater streams that gush valleywards, before the route heads for Rifugio Branca, belvedere par excellence, and a good place for lunch or refreshments. Waymarking comes as low poles topped with red/white paint stripes, cairns and upright stone markers, as well as yellow triangles.

From **Rifugio Forni** (2178m) walk down to the lowest car park and batch of signposts and bridge across **Torrente Frodolfo**. Then go up a stone staircase into conifer woods for the gentle climb SE – take care to follow signs for n.520 'Sentiero Glaciologico Alto' (not 'Basso') at the forks. Numerous side streams are crossed, and the slopes are shared with marmots and grazing cows that leave their messy signature along the way. As the trees thin, juniper and bilberry shrubs take over, and views extend up Val Cedèc crowned by Gran Zebrù (north). The path widens

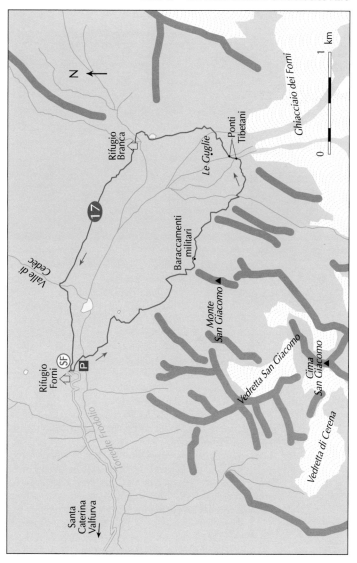

101

Crossing rocks smoothed by the glacier

and climbs almost imperceptibly thanks to the well-graded curves of an old military track that terminates at a ruined WWI encampment (**Baraccamenti militari**, 2520m). This affords splendid views northeast to Rifugio Branca and the summit triangle of Cevedale beyond. The path drops to ancient moraine ridges, long consolidated, and climbs again before being joined by a lower path ('Sentiero Glaciologico Basso') to cross a side stream. Soon you find yourself in a corridor of iron red rock, the surface pitted with holes left by ice-borne stones. The ensuing descent is like walking on the backs of rock whales.

The first of the **Ponti Tibetani** comes next (2500m, 1hr 50min). Then detour R on the peninsula between meltwater streams to one of the snouts of the glacier, and debris-covered moraine ridges close-up. Not far along the path is the second, longer bridge, followed by a descent over a smooth red rock outcrop, **Le Guglie**, then it is N along the other side of the valley. Up past a small lake and over a waterfall is **Rifugio Branca** (2487m, 40min), a superb belvedere with fine views of the combined glacial spread. A precipitous jeep track heads NW towards pasture and woodland, back to Rifugio Forni (2178m, 50min).

Ghiacciaio dei Forni is Italy's largest valley glacier. Nowadays the glacier snout is located around the 2500m mark, but 150 years ago it spread all the way down to the Rifugio Forni car park at 2100m, and during the period 1833–1864 it advanced at a rate of 26m a year. The gallery of fascinating photographs at the Forni refuge shows that it was all the rage for young couples and elegant ladies to go for an escorted stroll on the glacier itself, amid weird and wonderful sculptured pinnacles of ice. What is more, 10,000 years ago the combined Forni-Cedèc glaciers spilled down to occupy Valfurva and stretched all the way to Bormio. The Forni glacier has been monitored since 1895, with a retreat of 2km measured to date; it is 70–150 metres thick.

On the first bridge, not far from the glacier mouth

WALK 18
Valle di Cedèc

Start/Finish	Rifugio Forni
Distance	10.7km (6.6 miles)
Ascent/Descent	550m
Difficulty	Grade 1
Walking time	3hr 30min
Access	From Santa Caterina Valfurva a narrow 5.5km road climbs to Rifugio Forni and car parks. A jeep taxi service is also available.

Crowned by glaciated summits of rainbow-coloured rock, Valle di Cedèc is a magnet for walkers and mountaineers alike. The outward stretch of this route follows a stony jeep track across slopes pitted with marmot burrows, and the occupants make no secret of their presence, romping at play or on a quest for tasty wildflowers. The first objective is hospitable alpine Rifugio Pizzini in a breathtaking setting. The return is via a panoramic path with brilliant views to the immense Forni glacier. A delightful circuit with no difficulty at all but abundant, memorable views to take home.

This walk can also be used as the preface and tail-end to Walk 19, which visits high-altitude Rifugio Casati.

From **Rifugio Forni** (2178m) take the jeep track (n.528) that climbs NE at first around a shoulder into the broad valley, soon leaving the trees behind, the magnificence of Valle di Cedèc being revealed little by little with the ascent. The track transits through pasture for cows, nearing rushing **Torrente Cedèc** and a handful of picnic benches. It is a lengthy but problem-free haul to **Rifugio Pizzini** (2700m, 2hr), where the wonderful backdrop comprises cascading Vedretta Pasquale due east from Monte Pasquale, close to the Cevedale peaks east-southeast. But the undisputed king here is the elegant pyramid of Königspitze/Gran Zebrù north-northwest, its light grey rock distinguishing it from its red-brown neighbours, Punta Graglia and the low red mound of Cima

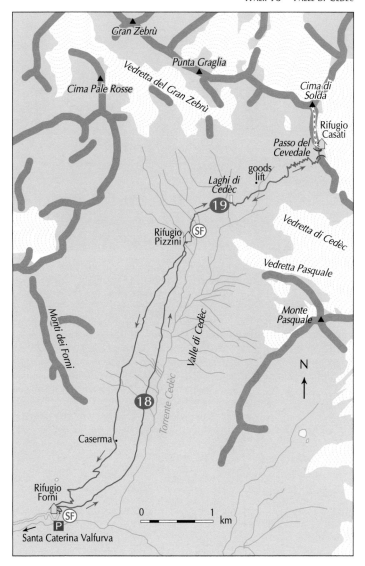

The immense Ghiacciaio dei Forni

Ancient moraine ridges colonised by plants and smoothed rock surfaces testify to the passage of glaciers long ago. An isolated boulder on the left of the path is a glacial erratic.

Pale Rosse, all surrounded by a sea of hanging glaciers (*vedrettas*) and colourful moraine spills.

Just below the refuge building cross the bridge and fork R on the panoramic route n.528, which crosses a series of small streams as it coasts along the western flanks of Valle di Cedèc, staying well above the jeep track. ◀ All the while the views are becoming more and more spectacular, with Pizzo Tresero southwest and its hanging glaciers, not far from the massive spread of Ghiacciaio dei Forni. Further along are the ruins of a WWI **Caserma** (2545m), trenches and stone walls another brilliant belvedere. Here begins the descent SW, past farm buildings and back to Rifugio Forni (2178m, 1hr 30min).

WALK 19
Rifugio Casati

Start/Finish	Rifugio Pizzini
Distance	8km (5 miles)
Ascent/Descent	560m
Difficulty	Grade 2–3
Walking time	3hr 30min + 1hr extension
Access	From Santa Caterina Valfurva a narrow 5.5km road climbs to Rifugio Forni and car parks; a jeep taxi service also covers this stretch, and runs as far as Rifugio Pizzini – otherwise allow 2hr on foot from Rifugio Forni to the walk start (see Walk 18).
Note	See map on page 105

This walk offers a superb day out in upper Valle di Cedèc amid breathtaking glacial landscapes and spectacular summits at the heart of the Stelvio National Park. The destination is one of the highest refuges in the whole of the park – 3254m Rifugio Casati. The whole day is spent in desolate surroundings, yet remarkably not devoid of life – ibex are easily spotted on rocky outcrops and brilliant clumps of golden creeping avens, purple saxifrage and pink-tinged glacier crowfoot accompany the walk to above the 3000m mark. A further panoramic summit, Cima di Solda, can be visited as an optional extension for amazing views down into the Sulden valley.

▸ Leave **Rifugio Pizzini** (2700m) on the jeep track (n.528) NE, soon crossing streams and an immense river of grey scree below Vedretta del Gran Zebrù. The track climbs steadily past the **Laghi di Cedèc** and soon past the **goods lift** loading point and power lines for Rifugio Casati – an outbuilding is visible on the dizzy ridge northeast, almost overhead. Now a path takes over, dropping into a basin of shattered red rock featuring flowers and another lake. Here commences the long zigzagging slog, both well trodden and well marked. Shortcuts are best avoided and plenty of awe-inspiring vistas provide an excuse for a breather. About halfway up are narrower and steeper sections needing extra care. Not far from the

In view of the high altitudes visited on this walk, it is advisable to wait until midsummer so as to avoid late-lying snow en route. Always wear warm windproof clothing.

The fantastic position of Rifugio Casati

top, rusty tangles of barbed wire left over from WWI are strewn around. **Passo del Cevedale** (3260m) is finally gained with its spectacular spread of snow and ice fields stretching to the Cevedale and beyond. Only a stroll away now is **Rifugio Casati** (3254m, 2hr).

Using material from an 1897 German-Austrian Alpine Club hut purposely destroyed at the end of WWI, **Rifugio Casati** was constructed in 1923 by the Casati family to commemorate their fallen soldier son. Now a key base for mountaineers, visitors flocked there in the 1960s and 70s for summer skiing thanks to lifts, now long gone. The helpful staff can provide equipment and the service of a qualified guide for any of the glacier traverses.

Extension to Cima di Solda (1hr return)
If the conditions are suitable and ice-free, this optional Grade 3 walkers' peak can be accessed by the path that strikes out NNW at the rear of Rifugio Casati, near the annex Rifugio Guasti. After a broad saddle, it zigzags up earth slopes to **Cima di Solda** (3376m). Watch your step on the return descent, especially in the presence of snow. Retrace your steps with care for the descent to Rifugio Pizzini (2700m, 1hr 30min).

WALK 20
Val Zebrù and Rifugio V° Alpini

Start/Finish	Baita del Pastore
Distance	9.2km (5.7 miles)
Ascent/Descent	750m
Difficulty	Grade 2–3
Walking time	4hr 25min + 20min extension
Access	In summer Perego buses run from Bormio via Madonna dei Monti as far as the Niblogo car park (1601m). From here, unless you walk (3hr), you will need the jeep taxi up to Baita del Pastore – they come and go continuously from July to early September. A sign at the Niblogo café-information point lists the authorised vehicles with contact phone numbers.
Note	Arrange with the taxi driver to be picked up afterwards if you do not intend to return on foot.

Val Zebrù runs west–east beneath a soaring ridge of awesome mountains. In places it is dramatically rugged and in others decidedly pastoral with flowered clearings and photogenically weathered timber chalets. Its dense forests are home to thriving populations of black grouse, red and roe deer, while chamois and ibex enjoy the higher rockscapes not far from the nests of eagles and bearded vultures. The best way to enjoy the magnificent valley is to stay a night either at idyllic Rifugio Campo, 2km downhill from the walk start, or up high at Rifugio V° Alpini amid dramatic rockscapes only minutes from the glacier.

The walk itself climbs – quite steeply at times – on scree and rough stones to explore the upper reaches of Vallon di Rio Marè, a branch of Val Zebrù. After the refuge, a traverse with some exposure leads into upper Val Zebrù to admire the multi-coloured moraines and Cima della Miniera, site of a long-abandoned iron ore mine.

It was in these desolate surroundings that feudal lord **Johannes Zebrusius**, the valley's namesake, ended his life in 1150. Returning home after a crusade to the Holy Land, he was heartbroken to find his beloved married to another and retired here in solitude.

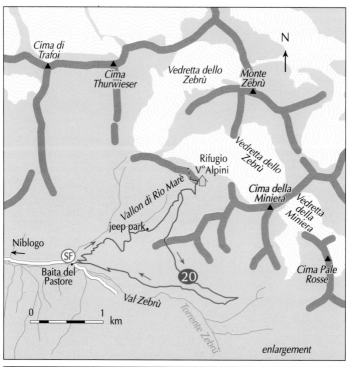

Leave **Baita del Pastore** (2166m) on the rough jeep track
(n.516) NE across grassy slopes studded with edelweiss.
Soon comes a problem-free encounter with a chaos of
shattered rock, the result of a colossal landslide – over
1 million cubic metres – that detached itself from Cima
Thurwieser (to the north) in September 2004. The way
continues across grassy slopes to the end of the track and
jeep parking area (2530m) where supplies are transferred
onto a motorised wheelbarrow. The hut itself is perched
dizzily above, still an awfully long way. High over cascading Rio Marè and alternating piste and path (follow
the 'boots' sign), you puff your way over light grey scree
dotted with Rhaetian poppies in the vast desolate rock
amphitheatre. For the time being ignore the turn-off for
Passo Zebrù and continue uphill past WWI terraces and
drystone walls to welcoming **Rifugio V° Alpini** (2878m,
2hr 10min).

> **Rifugio V° Alpini** is a well-run alpine refuge that
> dates back to 1884. It was later reconstructed and
> occupied by Italian forces during three consecutive
> winters in WWI; it takes its name from the V° – read
> as *quinto* (fifth) – battalion stationed there.

*The track traverses
the colossal 2004
landslide*

Extension to the glaciers (20min return)

Once you have your breath back, it is well worth finding the energy for this extension. Taking great care on the crumbly terrain, follow the 'ghiacciaio' signs past the solar panels and up to a saddle for the brilliant spectacle of slow spilling glaciers petering out into dark moraine at the foot of Monte Zebrù.

From Rifugio V° Alpini return downhill to the signed fork for Passo Zebrù at a prominent boulder (15min). Go L on the pleasant level path SSW where walkers are dwarfed on the immense scree slope. At a shoulder this rounds a corner, veering abruptly L (SE) to enter upper **Val Zebrù**. On a level for the most part the never-ending path continues in and out of folds in the terrain and minor streams, with occasional narrow stretches due to old rockfalls. A brief ascent concludes on easier grassy terrain and benches for contemplating the Cime dei Forni opposite to the south, as well as the rainbow moraines of the Vedretta della Miniera close at hand.

At a signed fork (2675m, 1hr) go R (W) in steady descent, crossing streams and flowered grassy slopes thick with black vanilla orchids and scented thyme, and past clumps of dwarf mountain pine. Far below flows **Torrente Zebrù**, which becomes a veritable river of gravel as you reach Baita del Pastore (2166m, 1hr).

Climb up at the rear of the refuge to see the glacier

WALK 21
Lago della Manzina

Start/Finish	Rifugio Forni
Distance	9km (5.6 miles)
Ascent/Descent	610m
Difficulty	Grade 1–2
Walking time	3hr 40min
Access	From Santa Caterina Valfurva a narrow 5.5km road climbs to Rifugio Forni and car parks. A jeep taxi service is also available.

In a high-altitude cirque well away from the bustle of the valley floor, Lago della Manzina is a good excuse for a rewarding walk with fantastic views to innumerable peaks and glaciers. En route playful marmots and birds of prey scanning the open mountainsides can be expected, as can a beautiful array of wildflowers, including brilliant blue gentians.

At the rear of **Rifugio Forni** (2178m) take the signed path NW up over polished rock slabs and past the tower-cum-stall onto grassy terrain thick with delicate eyebright flowers. You soon enter a beautiful wood of Arolla pine where your passage will undoubtedly be announced by a screeching nutcracker. Not far up fork L (W) on a wide track past a small **sluice gate**. Across the valley to the south Pizzo Tresero looms, draped with hanging glaciers high over Santa Caterina Valfurva, while southwest is the dark form of Monte Gavia.

The summer farms of **Pradaccio di sopra** are soon passed, and the level track cuts across open slopes with domes of juniper and heather, not to mention marmots. A stretch NW leads to the opening of **Valle della Manzina** and the signed turn-off (2360m, 50min) where you fork R (N) on n.575 for the start of the climb in the company of cascading streams draped with delicate star jasmine. Fat blue bellflowers and gentians accompany the winding path up to a cirque housing tiny **Lago Prealda**. An earth crest is

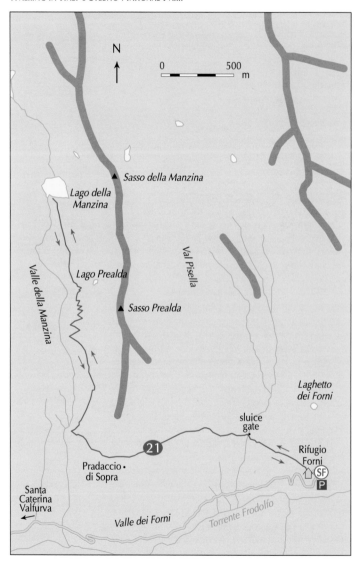

followed for the continuing ascent, artistic cairns showing the way up to the vast amphitheatre where a waterfall cascades into **Lago della Manzina** (2784, 1hr 30min). ▶ High above are the Cime dei Forni peaks to the north, with Cima della Manzina and Monte Confinale northwest.

After a rest and picnic, point your boots downhill, but take your time as – clouds permitting – a fantastic treat is in store in the shape of awe-inspiring views of the Forni glacier (east) and the complete line-up of summits from Palon de la Mare to Pizzo Tresero. Return to the wide track and back to Rifugio Forni (2178m, 1hr 20min).

This is a lovely, solitary spot, with green lichen stained stones, purple primulas and daisies.

Pizzo Tresero looms across the valley

WALK 22

Santa Caterina to Sant'Antonio

Start	Santa Caterina Valfurva
Finish	Sant'Antonio Valfurva
Distance	17km (10.6 miles)
Ascent	650m
Descent	1050m
Difficulty	Grade 1–2
Walking time	5hr 40min
Access	Santa Caterina and Sant'Antonio are on the Perego bus line from Bormio.
Note	At Santa Caterina, the officially waymarked start of the Ables route is located on a surfaced road 200m back along the Bormio road. However, the walk start described here uses a lovely old path, much preferable; the two unite about 20min uphill.

This is a long and lovely traverse along the northeastern flanks of Valfurva, and can easily be shortened to suit individual whims. Starting with an easy climb, it alternates stretches of woodland with manmade clearings traditionally known as *maggenghi*, of key importance for pasture and haymaking. It touches on the working summer farm and popular eatery Agriturismo Ables, where a good lane can be followed back to Santa Caterina if so desired (allow 2hr 50min total). The main route proceeds on a level, mostly across open grassed slopes, where kestrel and golden eagle hunt. At the Confinale di sopra farm, a series of marked paths lead back to Santa Caterina (total 5hr), but it is worth continuing all the way to the Baita Cavallaro huts, which perch on the beautiful southern edge of Val Zebrù. In conclusion, lanes lead down to Sant'Antonio, for the bus back to the start.

At **Santa Caterina** (1740m), opposite Hotel Compagnoni and alongside the building housing the tourist office, take the unmarked path that leads diagonally uphill for the first of many broad zigzags through pine wood. Ignore forks and stick to the well-trodden route to Speluga (1856m) and its rusty shed. Not far up you join a lane where signs

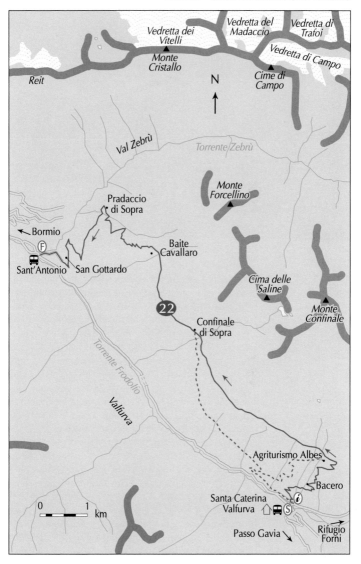

The path crosses meadows

In the clearings, sunbaked slopes harbour bright houseleeks and pungent thyme.

now point you R across a stream. A string of timber chalets in differing states of repair, each set amid panoramic, manicured meadows punctuate the lovely ascent. After **Bacero** (1986m), the way narrows to a good path, climbing above the tree line with the exception of scattered Arolla pines like sentinels. There are now uninterrupted views to Pizzo Tresero (southeast) and Monte Sobretta (southwest). At the 2200m junction (1hr 30min) it is only a matter of minutes L to **Agriturismo Albes** (2233m), but for the main route fork R to join the higher path n.527 near more chalets. Signs here point you L (NW) for the path traversing above Ables and past a waterfall, on lengthy muddy stretches churned up by cows.

The livestock are finally left behind and you can relax and admire the views, as well as the lilac pinks that add colour and scent to the open grassy slopes. The path WNW widens across silvery rock slabs colonised by conifer woods with nutcrackers galore, and benches dot the way. ◄ A gentle ascent out of the wood affords good views southeast to pyramidal Corno dei Tre Signori. Next comes the pastoral basin housing a waterfall and modest summer farm **Confinale di Sopra** (2288m, 1hr 45min).

(To return to Santa Caterina fork L downhill here and follow signs.)

Stick to the high route, now a lane NNW looking
to the majestic Reit crest above Bormio. ▸ On pasture
slopes stand the **Baite Cavallaro** huts (2168m, 40min)
with gorgeous views north to Monte Cristallo, Cime di
Campo and even some snow and the uppermost ski lifts
linked with Passo dello Stelvio. Miles below (due W) lies
the triangle of Bormio at the confluence of three valleys.

Now brace your knees for the steep lane plunging SW
through cool forest to reach the pastoral idyll of **Pradaccio
di Sopra** (1744m). Follow signs for Sant'Antonio, L, and
across a bridge – ignore the lower unmarked fork and
keep L around a corner above a line of old houses. The
ensuing descent is gentle and looks over terraced slopes.
The hamlet of **San Gottardo** is finally reached, and a
short stretch of tarmac leads to the main road and bus
stop at **Sant'Antonio** (1358m, 1hr 45min).

The Valfurva villages

Further on the trees
assume curious
sculpted forms, the
outcome of assiduous
munching by
livestock.

WALK 23

Monte delle Scale

Start/Finish	Lago delle Scale
Distance	5km (3 miles)
Ascent/Descent	570m
Difficulty	Grade 1–2
Walking time	3hr
Access	The Perego bus bound for Cancano comes up here from Bormio in summer. Car drivers – be aware that the road has countless hairpin bends and is very narrow.

Monte delle Scale is an unassuming twin-peaked mountain, not especially high but rising vertiginously close to Bormio. Standing isolated, it is very easy to reach on foot and gives a spectacular 360° panorama to the glaciated heart of the Ortler-Cevedale group. The views also take in the two Cancano lakes, dammed in the 1940–1950s for hydroelectricity.

The walk is extremely enjoyable and straightforward, with the exception of a short rock gully passage that rates Grade 2. A couple of hospitable eateries and modest guesthouses are located near the walk start, as are the Torri di Fraele. These medieval watchtowers were essential in the defence of Bormio and an ancient trade route that passed an impervious passage where wooden steps fixed to the cliff could be removed if necessary.

From the northern end of fishing reserve **Lago delle Scale** (1931m) set out on clearly marked path n.197. This enters a wood of dwarf mountain pine and alpenrose, with continuous views down to the two Cancano lakes and their respective dams. The Stelvio Pass road can soon be seen to the northeast, complete with tortuous twists and turns. The path leaves the cover of trees, reaching a couple of benches, before embarking on a wide curve R to cross a modest gully, where a little scrambling is required. The path quickly improves and ascends grassy slopes thick with white mountain avens to a broad **saddle** (2431m, 1hr 30min) and picnic area

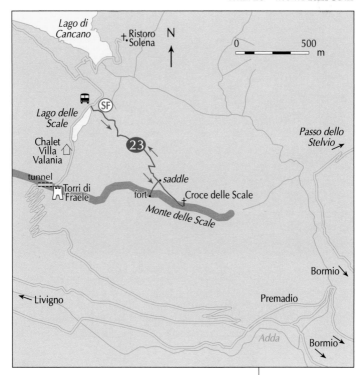

with information boards. Nearby are platforms for artillery while to your R is the opening for the amazing WWI **tunnel-fort** leading through to the southern side of Monte delle Scale, and dizzy views.

> The isolated position of Monte delle Scale made it a logical choice for **artillery placements** during WWI as they could set their sights on the Stelvio Pass and the front line. A remarkable fort was hewn out within the mountain and can still be visited, with the help of information boards in English and Italian. The premises have been partially rebuilt with concrete for safety reasons.

Lago Cancano, dammed in the 1940–1950s for hydroelectricity

Return to the saddle and fork R for the final climb – a little exposed at times – to **Croce delle Scale** (2501m, 15min), belvedere par excellence! As well as a gigantic cross that is lit up at night-time, there are breathtaking views across a host of Stelvio summits, including the Ortler.

Watching your step, return to the 2431m saddle and then to Lago delle Scale (1931m, 1hr 15min).

WALK 24
Valle Forcola Traverse

Start	IV Cantoniera
Finish	Ristoro Solena, Cancano
Distance	12km (7.5 miles)
Ascent/Descent	300m/900m
Difficulty	Grade 1–2
Walking time	3hr 30min
Access	The summer Perego bus from Bormio to Passo dello Stelvio/ Stilfser Joch stops at IV Cantoniera, close to Passo Umbrail and the Swiss border. At the end of the walk, catch the summer Perego bus back to Bormio.
Note	The 'IV Cantoniera' is the fourth ('quarta') of the buildings for road maintenance crews.

This is a longish traverse from the vicinity of the famous Stelvio Pass and opens with a marvellous panoramic stretch to Bocchetta di Forcola, a first-rate lookout that assumed strategic importance during WWI, on the border of neutral Switzerland. After exploring trenches and fortifications, the walk descends into Valle Forcola, ducking behind Monte Braulio on mule tracks of military origin. It concludes at a welcoming café-restaurant, Ristoro Solena, close to the shores of the Cancano lakes, dammed in the 1940–1950s for hydroelectricity. A recommended variant breaks off just after Bocchetta di Forcola to circle the lovely high-altitude Piano di Pedenolo plateau on old military tracks, rejoining the main route in lower Valle Forcola.

The walk is served by buses at start and finish and contains no difficulty, and is popular with Italian and Swiss mountainbikers who zip back and forth between countries.

From the bus stop at the **IV Cantoniera** (2503m) walk N on the minor road in the direction of **Passo Umbrail**, and then branch L on signed path n.145. This is a gentle climb W over grassed slopes ablaze with wildflowers such as black vanilla orchids, lilac asters and golden alpine ragwort, in the company of marmots and grazing cows. There are constant magnificent views across to the

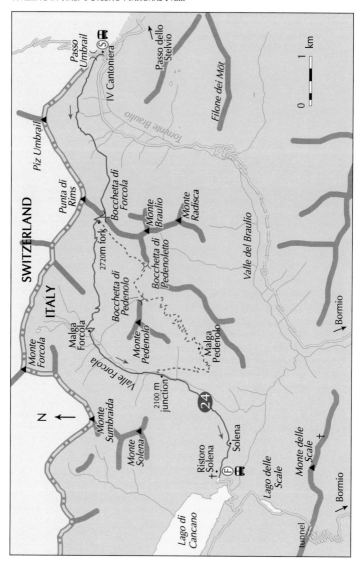

Filone dei Möt crest (south) backed by glaciated Monte Cristallo, Monte Braulio ahead southwest and the light grey ridge of Piz Umbrail overhead, marking the border with Switzerland. ▸

A final decisive ascent and you gain the warren of trenches and wartime caverns of **Bocchetta di Forcola** (2760m, 1hr 15min) also known as Forcola di Rims, a broad saddle linking Monte Braulio and Punta di Rims. Back east-southeast the massive Ortler summit is visible beyond Passo dello Stelvio, while Monte Scorluzzo and Cristallo can be admired to the east. Ahead elegant light grey Monte Sumbraida dominates Valle Forcola.

Take the wide track N at first for the beginning of the descent. It quickly reaches a wartime barracks (2741m) on bare lunar terrain, before making its way W past a **2720m fork** (see variant) and into the centre of **Valle Forcola** on a swathe of green amid swarming marmot colonies. Down past disused farm **Malga Forcola** (2313m, 1hr) and its modest waterfall the valley is squeezed in and the landscape becomes decidedly rockier with scree flows like avalanches. ▸ The track broadens, alongside a growing stream, to the junction where the variant route slots back in at 2100m.

At Bocchetta di Forcola

En route, walkers are inevitably treated to acrobatic aerial displays by the huge resident flock of alpine choughs, and the antics of the many marmot colonies.

Carpets of white mountain avens do their best to colonise the loose stones.

Wartime barracks in Valle Forcola

Piano di Pedenolo variant (2hr 30min)

From the 2720m fork turn L (SW) on n.146 for the traverse via **Bocchetta di Pedenoletto** (2790m) then **Bocchetta di Pedenolo** (2704m). Downhill in wide bends that hint of military origin, you cross panoramic pasture flats dotted with dolina depressions to reach **Malga Pedenolo** (2386m). Then you need the track due N down steep mountainside to a bridge where the main route n.145 is picked up at the **2100m junction**.

Next door is a church commemorating the victims of both the war and the construction work on the Cancano dams.

Dense spreads of dwarf mountain pine, colonisers of the rugged slopes, accompany the track as it bears SSW, high above a vertiginous gorge and the stream and with a good view south to Monte delle Scale. At the **Solena** (1975m) junction and picnic area keep straight on (W) over a rise for the final leg to **Ristoro Solena** (1954m, 1hr 15min) and the bus stop. ◄

WALK 25
Monte Scorluzzo and Filone dei Möt

Start	Passo dello Stelvio
Finish	III Cantoniera
Distance	9km (5.6 miles)
Ascent	350m
Descent	850m
Difficulty	Grade 3
Walking time	3hr 30min
Access	Perego buses from Bormio serve Passo dello Stelvio/Stilfser Joch in summer. SAD buses come up from the Gomagoi side.
Note	The 'III (terza) Cantoniera' is the third of the road maintenance buildings.

This is arguably the most spectacular walk in this guidebook, spending all day on superbly panoramic ridges, a stone's throw from vast glacier spreads. Clear weather is essential for both visibility and safety, as lengthy sections are moderately exposed. To avoid the added difficulty of snow and ice, it is advisable to wait until summer is well under way. In any case go equipped for the altitude – around the 3000m mark for several hours – with warm clothes, plenty of drinking water and food.

Even if the complete route is out of your comfort zone, do visit Monte Scorluzzo, a straightforward Grade 2 ascent – allow 2hr for the return trip. Furthermore, the walk is easily transformed into a complete circuit returning to Passo dello Stelvio – allow 4hr 15min.

At **Passo dello Stelvio** (2758m), a short way downhill from the *funivia* (cable car) station where the bus stops, signs point you L (S) onto a rough lane which wastes no time in ascending. At **Passo delle Platigliole** (2908m) you fork R (W) onto a steeper path that winds its way across dark rock debris and old trenches amid clumps of glacier crowfoot and creeping avens, concluding at **Monte Scorluzzo** (3094m, 1hr) with its summit cross.

Once you have your breath back and photographed what feels like the top of the world, with 360° views that

The amazing panorama from Monte Scorluzzo

include Piz Bernina to the W, take the faint red/white marked path to the L of the cross. Heading SE it clambers down over rocks; extra care is a must due to the exposure and possibly slippery surfaces. Watch out for your rucksack on overhangs. A couple of lengths of guiding hand chain are reassuring. After some time the path widens somewhat and the gradient eases as a crest with information panels is gained (15min). South-southeast extends the glittering glacier on Monte Cristallo with its summertime ski pistes, while below is the curious light grey pitted limestone of the Platigliole, home to ibex. Continue to the **Osservatorio italiano** (2926m) set amid rusty barbed wire and splintered planks from wartime huts. Steps lead to a saddle where an original wartime path is followed W along the **Filone dei Möt** ridge, dizzily high over the Pian di Scorluzzo and its tiny lakes under Le Rese ridge. ◄

The views are breathtaking, and the open terrain is the ideal hunting ground for birds of prey.

Further down, a **2768m junction** (1hr) denotes the entrance to the **Villaggio Militare** set on a stunningly scenic outcrop in a protected position high above the Stelvio road and Valle del Braulio.

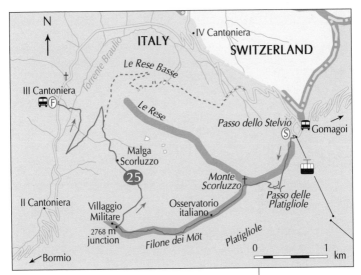

During WWI both the road pass and Monte Scorluzzo were under Austrian control and

The Villaggio Militare

STILFSER JOCH/PASSO DELLO STELVIO

The great military road over the Stilfser-joch or Monte Stelvio, now turns to the right, up the north side of a ravine, descending from the westward, and opposite to an enormous and precipitous pile of rock, forming the shoulder of the Madatsch-berg. After clearing the first angle of the mountain by following its windings, you arrive at a small inn from whence the eye commands the depth and termination of the ravine before you, and the whole course of this astonishing route to the summit of the ridge, in a series of interminable zigzags lessening in the perspective...The greater portion of the last league presented a singular and astonishing example of human labour. Half the road is covered in by strongly constructed wooden galleries, with roofs and supports sufficiently massive to resist the pressure of descending avalanches...

The Pedestrian, a Summer's Ramble in the Tyrol (1832) Charles Joseph Latrobe

Stilfser Joch/Passo dello Stelvio is located at 2758m above sea level, and until 1936 was the highest road pass in the world. A mammoth civil engineering task, the idea was first conceived in 1812 but had to wait until the fall of Napoleon when the area was restored to Austro-Hungarian control and Emperor Franz Joseph I determined to link Germany and the Tyrol with Milan. It was constructed in 21 months between 1820 and 1825. On the eastern side it boasts a mind-boggling 48 hairpin bends and an average gradient of 100:9 above Gomagoi (1273m), then 38 bends, a couple of tunnels and a 100:13.5 gradient to Bormio (1217m) in the west. Along the way were the *cantoniere*, inns to house road crews and provide food and change of horses. The road was even kept open in the winter months for horse-drawn sleighs until 1848 (nine hours was a normal journey time in the snow) but now it is only passable from June to October. It is wholly in Italy nowadays. Buses run up from both sides – a memorable experience – and hotel accommodation is plentiful. From 2013, a toll will be levied on motorists on the Südtirol side (see www.greenpass.bz.it).

The pass has the air of a festive bazaar, with colourful stands selling souvenirs and hot dogs, to the delight of intrepid cyclists and motorbikers who mingle with the summer skiers intent on the slopes and lifts which have been allowed to despoil the splendid glaciers and snowfields since the 1960s. Last but not least, the Stilfser Joch is an important watershed between the River Adige, which descends via Verona to end up in the Adriatic Sea, and the Adda which flows via Lake Como to eventually join the mighty Po River.

equipped with cannons (which bombarded Bormio in the closing year of the war, 1918), so the Italians dug in on the adjoining Filone dei Möt ridge. The **Villaggio Militare** was a real home away from home for the alpine troops stationed at these elevated altitudes. The maze of stone huts, castle-like constructions and well graded walkways have been restored and helpful information panels installed. Allow extra time to explore and savour the place.

From the junction a narrowish path marked with red/white poles and paint splashes descends quickly NE in the company of carpets of alpine daisies. It peters out crossing broken rock so set your sights on the large cairn set on grassy terrain ahead. There head NW across a sea of golden flowers from low pole to low pole – joining the dots as it were – to the abandoned yet sturdy stone barn of **Malga Scorluzzo** (2531m, 30min), looking north to Piz Umbrail. A former military lane leads easily NNW in the company of marmots to a Y-junction (2483m, 15min) where a variant heads back to Passo dello Stelvio.

Return to Passo dello Stelvio (1hr 30min)
Keep straight ahead (N) on the lane in gentle ascent. This curves E via **Le Rese Basse** (2644m) before joining the road for a final leg to Passo dello Stelvio (2758m).

Fork L on the long curves of the lane (shortcuts possible) that finally reach the valley floor, **Torrente Braulio** and power lines. Across the bridge, cut straight up the grassy banks to the dark red building of the **III Cantoniera** (2326m, 30min) and bus stop on the roadside. ▸

Not far away is a small church, cemetery and WWI memorial.

WALK 26
Goldseeweg

Start	Stilfser Joch/Passo dello Stelvio
Finish	Trafoi
Distance	14km (8.7 miles)
Ascent	100m
Descent	1350m
Difficulty	Grade 2
Walking time	4hr 10min
Access	Stilfser Joch/Passo dello Stelvio can be reached by midsummer SAD bus from Gomagoi via Trafoi. You can also get there from Bormio thanks to the Perego service. The bus stop is at the funivia (cable car).

A brilliant way to start – or a satisfying way to conclude – a walking holiday, this justifiably popular route leaves you inebriated with visions of majestic glaciers and soaring peaks, culminating in the massive Ortler. Beginning at the dramatic Stelvio Pass, the Goldseeweg wanders through WWI sites before descending ever so gradually along the upper edge of the Trafoi valley. Walkers have ample time to appreciate the magnificent scenery, along with wildflower posies of glacier crowfoot, chamois ragwort and masses of gentians.

The only restrictions for this walk are those posed by the weather – low clouds and adverse conditions mean no views, while limit-of-season snowfalls may close the road. Whatever the month, wrap up warm as chilly winds are the norm on these high-altitude paths. From Furkelhütte you can ride the chairlift down to Trafoi if you choose – cutting 1hr 20min off the walk time, and 600m in descent.

At **Stilfser Joch/Passo dello Stelvio** (2758m) walk L (Bormio direction) past the stalls hung with indescribable souvenirs to the easy broad path that forks R up earth banks thick with glacier crowfoot. Not far up keep R on n.20 below fortress-like **Rifugio Garibaldi** (2838m) on Drei Sprachen Spitze ('three languages peak'), the old frontier between Romansch-speaking Switzerland, Italy

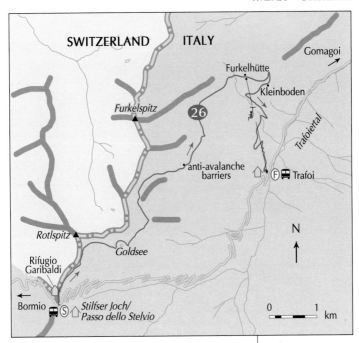

and German-speaking Tyrol. The clear path coasts NNE at first, past stone ruins, scattered buildings and information boards (in German and Italian) attesting to the presence of a WWI Austrian stronghold with barracks, a hospital and even electricity. After rounding a point, it descends gently, soon cutting E across the red detritus of a rock glacier beneath **Rotlspitz**, and passes pond-like **Goldsee** (2708m) to a ruined fort occupying a strategic corner.

The scenic route proceeds NE, mostly on a level, in the company of skittery sheep and occasional patches of old snow covering the rock-earth terrain. At old **anti-avalanche barriers** (2530m) the refuge and chairlift finally come into view, still a long way below. This spot is an excellent lookout north to Vinschgau backed by the Ötztaler Alps with the Weisskugel northeast. There

Stilfser Joch/Passo dello Stelvio where the walk begins

is an impressive line-up of ice and rock to the south, too: standing out are Geister Spitze (the 'ghost peak', so-called because the spirit of a Trafoi shepherd is said to wander the summit at night), the massive central dark Madatsch outcrop, the curious Nashornspitze (supposedly named by the children of Trafoi for the innkeeper's 'nose') then the Ortler to the southeast, its snow slopes dotted with roped climbing groups.

> Soaring 3905m high, **the Ortler** in German – or Ortles in Italian – is the loftiest peak in the Stelvio National Park, as well as the highest in the Alps east of Piz Bernina. It was first scaled back in 1804 by a chamois hunter Joseph Pichler, on behalf of the Archduke of Austria.
>
> The name derives from Ortnit or Ortwin, the Ladin founder of a farmhouse high in the Sulden valley. However, in German 'Ort' means 'place', and according to legend, the mountain was the dwelling place of the souls of Celtic princes and pagan gods. But the most popular story stars Ortler the big-headed giant. Irritated by his taller neighbours Königspitze and Cevedale, he puffed himself

up to gain extra metres. But taunted by a crafty dwarf who climbed on to his head, out of fury he froze into the solid mountain we see today.

From 1916 until the end of the WWI hostilities, the summit itself was occupied. Tunnels and an ice cave were excavated to house 30 men, and two hefty cannons were dragged up.

The descent finally begins in earnest now, with steep stretches over stony pasture where black vanilla orchids flourish, and into beautiful conifer woods. A tree-sculpted figure stands guard by the path on the last stage to cows and slopes cleared for winter skiing, then alpine café **Furkelhütte/Rifugio Forcola** (2153m, 2hr 50min), which boasts enviable views. It also has a handy chairlift down to Trafoi.

On foot, n.17 takes the dirt road R (E). At an information board by all means cut R down the slope to **Kleinboden**, a former WWI ammunition store (the official path curves N before swinging back S, taking a little longer). A well-trodden path now plunges S into cool, quiet conifer woods, crisscrossing under the chairlift. Once across a plank bridge, n.17 follows a forestry lane then a ski piste – keep your eyes skinned for an arrow L where the path resumes. Further down this joins another lane (n.4). As it reaches Hotel Madaccio, fork L down to the chairlift station at Trafoi (1532m, 1hr 20min).

Wonderful views to the Ortler

WALK 27
Berglhütte

Start/Finish	Trafoi Visitor Centre
Distance	12.5km (7.7 miles)
Ascent/Descent	645m
Difficulty	Grade 1–2
Walking time	4hr (6hr with extension)
Access	Trafoi can be reached by SAD bus in summer. From the bus stop it is a short walk uphill past Hotel Bella Vista to the Naturtrafoi Visitor Centre. By car it is possible drive to the parking area near the Drei Brunnen sanctuary – a saving of 1hr 30min.

An exciting walk to a superbly placed refuge makes a wonderful day out for all the family. It follows a straightforward path that gives vast views over the upper Trafoi valley with a host of glaciated peaks around the dramatic Stelvio Pass, not to mention the famous road itself. Walkers with extra stamina and with experience on narrow paths and moderately exposed terrain can extend this route into an excellent Grade 3 circuit that puffs up to 2580m, before a drawn-out 1000m descent all the way to Trafoi.

From the **Visitor Centre** at Trafoi (1543m), follow signs for the path past the **church** and across fields S. From the start the views upvalley are magnificent, with a clutch of light grey peaks cradling glaciers that pour their icy contents valleywards. A minor surfaced road takes you to the **campsite**, which you skirt R then immediately L (S) through conifer forest. Further on this crosses a first bridge over **Trafoier Bach** to curve past disused red-roofed buildings (former **Caserma Scuola Alpina**) to a **car park** (1594m, 50min) and picnic-BBQ area with a map-board. Here fork L across the second bridge and soon to the long third bridge leading across to the **Drei Brunnen sanctuary** (1605m), beautifully positioned near the base of the breathtaking Madatsch outcrop.

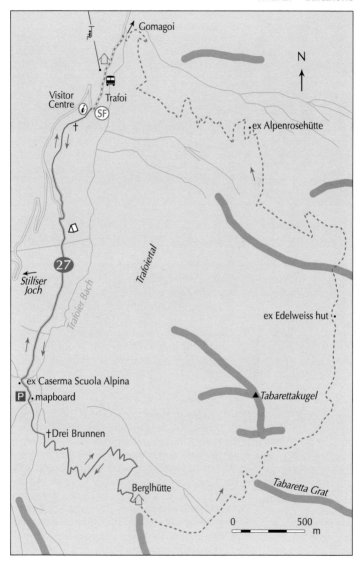

The bridge to Drei Brunnen backed by the Madatsch

The **Drei Brunnen sanctuary** is a tiny, atmospheric Baroque church nestling in woodland. It originated from 'three springs' spouting miraculous holy water. A host of fascinating 'ex voto' paintings decorate the walls. Ancient and modern, they attest to the devotion of the mountain folk and their gratitude to the Holy Mother for her intervention in difficult circumstances such as illness or outright danger such as avalanches.

Here path n.15 begins its steady climb SE through woodland. Marvellously contorted Arolla pines spread their roots across the path and well-placed benches offer a panoramic spot to pause en route – the views are impressive and ever-improving, with the tight zigzags of the Stelvio road incising the grassy slopes opposite. As the path makes a wide swing through a thicket of dwarf mountain pines, the magnificent Tabaretta Spitze comes into sight ahead to the east. Further up, and just above the tree line – thus ensuring uninterrupted views – stands **Berglhütte** (2188m, 1hr 30min) on the lower extremity of the massive northwest spur of the giant Ortler. ◄

This is a gorgeous spot to enjoy an alfresco lunch and scrutinise the views with the help of the huge set of binoculars provided.

Berglhütte, also known as Rifugio Borletti, is a key gateway for ascents of the 3905m Ortler. It has a long history stretching back to 1884 when it was built by members of the German-Austrian Alpine Club who named it Hamburger-Hütte. Post-WWI it was assigned to the Milano branch of the Italian Alpine Club who rebuilt it twice – in the aftermath of both wars; ownership was recently transferred to the Bozen Province. As there is no cableway here the hut relies on rare helicopter drops for its supplies, as well as the capacious backpacks of its cheery staff.

Unless you opt for the extension, return the same way to the sanctuary and car park (1hr), and from there to Trafoi (1543m, 40min).

Extension to Trafoi via Edelweiss Hut (3hr 40min)

At the rear of Berglhütte (2188m) take path n.18 for the traverse E across steep grey moraine in a vast cirque well below the Ortler. Not far along is a tricky section where the stream often washes gravel away – watch your step. In magnificent surroundings the path bears NE, climbing steadily to a 2440m shoulder, the **Tabaretta Grat**. A little more ascent awaits – ignore n.18 that branches R for Tabarettascharte – and keep due N on n.18A for the junction marked by the derelict **Edelweiss Hut** (2481m).

From here on you follow n.19 which soon begins its never-ending descent-cum-plunge. Curving N across the last scree it reaches terrain anchored by scraggly dwarf mountain pines, soon joined by larch and Arolla pines providing a soft carpet of needles, welcome underfoot. Ruined **Alpenrosehütte** (2029m) marks the start of a long-established forest, and while the path is easy the roots and rocks can be slippery if wet. You finally reach the valley floor and are directed across the stream to Trafoi (1543m).

WALK 28
Trafoi Waterfalls

Start/Finish	Trafoi Visitor Centre
Distance	7.5km (4.6 miles)
Ascent/Descent	250m
Difficulty	Grade 1–2
Walking time	2hr 50min
Access	Trafoi can be reached by SAD bus in the summer. From the bus stop walk uphill past Hotel Bella Vista to the Naturtrafoi Visitor Centre. By car, you could drive as far as the parking area near the Drei Brunnen sanctuary, cutting 1hr 30min off the total time.

A popular walk for family groups, this climbs up by three torrential waterfalls in the Trafoi valley. Here at the foot of the awesome Madatsch, a natural amphitheatre resounds with crashing water from the many torrents swollen with glacial meltwater. The first fall visited spurts amazingly out of a slit in the mountainside, while the second all but soaks walkers who forget their rain jackets and go too slowly – to the delight of youngsters. Apart from a couple of narrow stretches where you need to watch your step, it is a straightforward route, and gives lovely views down to the valley floor. The picnic and BBQ area alongside the Trafoier Bach river is a lovely place to while away an afternoon.

From the **Visitor Centre** at Trafoi (1543m) follow signs for the well-trodden path past the church and across fields S. Further along this is surfaced. At the **campsite** skirt R then L for the minor road through conifer forest. Across a bridge it curves past disused buildings (the former **Caserma Scuola Alpina**) to a **car park** (1594m, 50min) and picnic-BBQ area preceding a **mapboard** and second bridge. Ignore the third bridge to the Drei Brunnen sanctuary, and instead fork R on path n.9. This heads S through thickets of dwarf mountain pine, following the right bank of the gushing torrent in its broad grey gravel bed. Towering ahead is the Madatsch outcrop, while the

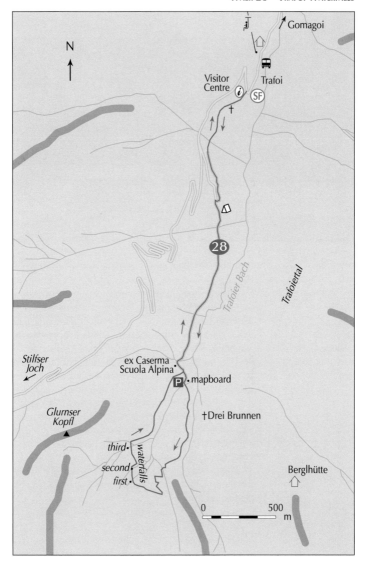

Views down the Trafoi valley from the ascent path

Wonderful bird's-eye views back to the valley floor can be enjoyed.

walk route and the three waterfalls can be seen clearly below it.

The way leads across blinding white scree to cross a second torrent that emerges from a cleft canyon choked with rocks. Tight zigzags lead up through wood of rowan and green alder brightened by columbines and pink alpenrose. ◀

The **first waterfall** is finally reached, spouting from its rock slit. Not far on is the **second**; the path passes behind it, a cooling shower awaits! In descent now, the path is soon aided by a guiding cable over rocks to the **third fall**. Further stretches of cable help you down more rocks, then steps take over. Back into the wood, it is past a wildlife area and back to the mapboard and car park (1hr 20min). Turn L to return to Trafoi (40min). (Turn-offs beckon walkers into the wood on this final stretch; while these mean avoiding the tarmac, be aware that lengthy detours are involved.)

WALK 29
Tabarettahütte

Start/Finish	Old church, Sulden
Distance	9km (5.6 miles)
Ascent/Descent	700m
Difficulty	Grade 1–2
Walking time	4hr 15min + 2hr 30min extension
Access	Sulden/Solda has year-round SAD bus links via Gomagoi with Spondinig/Spondigna and trains.

Gigantic waves of moraine and the overriding presence of the Ortler are the flavour of the day on this superb walk above the resort village of Sulden. The paths run along the foot of the north face of the looming giant, human figures mere pinpoints in the immensity and starkness of the landscape. Colourful spots come as dark green foliage and white blooms of mountain avens, an excellent moraine coloniser and consolidator. From Tabarettahütte, the objective of the walk, fit walkers who feel at home on exposed ridges will enjoy the spectacular Grade 3 extension to Payerhütte. Erected in 1875 by the Prague branch of the German-Austrian Alpine Club, it was named after Julius Payer, an Austrian officer cartographer and first to climb at least 36 of the summits over 3000m in the Ortler region.

At **Sulden** (1860m), at the rear of Hotel Eller and close to the old church, well-used path n.4 strikes out WSW on a gentle uphill gradient through beautiful conifer woods and a monument to Stübl who constructed the Payerhütte. All of a sudden it emerges from the trees onto stony terrain in view of blinding ridges of moraine, above which looms the Ortler, with the two refuges both visible due W close to Tabaretta Spitze. Joined by a path from the Langenstein chairlift you move W, crossing a jeep track to a shoulder green with dwarf mountain pines. After a further stretch on old moraine (**Marltmorane**) is a boulder plastered with plaques for mountaineers who lost their lives on the Ortler. Nearby is the **n.8 junction** (2386m) where the return route forks off.

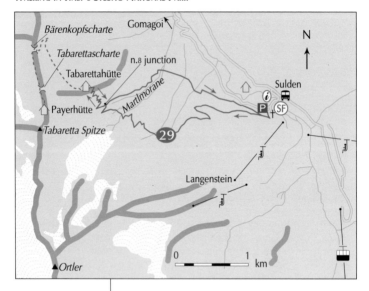

For the time being, keep upwards for the stiff never-ending zigzags NW past sheep intent on grazing and oblivious to the grandiose views. Comfortable **Tabarettahütte/Rifugio Tabaretta** (2556m, 2hr 15min) and its popular sun terrace occupy a commanding position surveying the whole of the Suldental, directly beneath Payerhütte on its impossible perch. Clear well-trodden paths proceed upwards.

Extension to Payerhütte (2hr 30min return)

A constantly narrowing grey scree path, slippery at times, n.4 cuts NW up a slope flanked by a gaping drop. With the ascent come ever-improving views of the thick sculpted layers of snow and ice on the Ortler. A series of tight zigzags lead to the first saddle in the rugged ridge, **Bärenkopfscharte/Forcella dell'Orso** (Bear's Head Pass, 2871m). Here the path moves to the other side of the crest, ascending due S amid weathered light-coloured rock needles and towers testifying to the presence of dolomite. Take care your rucksack does not catch on overhanging rocks. A section hewn into the rock and aided with a steel cable leads to **Tabarettascharte/ Passo della Tabaretta** (2903m) with superb views to the Stelvio Pass road snaking ahead. A final leg along an airy stretch concludes at **Payerhütte/Rifugio Payer** (3029m, 1hr 30min), a spectacular belvedere, and essential base for mountaineers en route to the Ortler. Return the same way – taking extra special care – to Tabarettahütte (2556m, 1hr).

Retrace your steps down the zigzags to the boulder and the n.8 junction (2386m, 30min) and fork L on this little-frequented path. Essentially NE, on its quest down and down, it alternates moraines (watch your step on loose stones) and wooded mountain slopes. At 1950m you are finally signed R (E) through dwarf mountain pine thickets and a lovely view northeast to the Vertain. At junctions follow signs for Sulden (n.8), joining the Kulturpromenade lined with benches. At the memorial to Stübl, you rejoin n.4 to the old church at Sulden (1hr 30min).

Path through dwarf mountain pines

WALK 30
Hintergrathütte Tour

Start/Finish	Old church, Sulden
Distance	15km (9.3 miles)
Ascent/Descent	850m
Difficulty	Grade 2–3
Walking time	5hr
Access	Sulden/Solda has year-round SAD bus links via Gomagoi with Spondinig/Spondigna and trains.
Note	Both the start and end of the walk can be shortened by using the Langenstein chairlift and the cable car.

Hintergrathütte (also known as Rifugio al Coston) is easily the best-placed hut in the Stelvio National Park. Perched on a crest 1000m above the Sulden valley, it faces the breathtaking spectacle of frozen cascades of ice and snow on Monte Zebrù and the magnificent Königspitze (see Walk 32). Seeing is believing and getting there is half the fun, with the majestic Ortler dominating the opening leg.

The walk has two Grade 3 stretches: between the Langenstein chairlift and Hintergrathütte where the traverse is narrow and exposed at times, then from the intermediate cable car to the valley floor due to the steepness. In both cases the 'worst' bits have cables and chains for reassurance. To visit Hintergrathütte on an easier (Grade 2) path, take n.12 from the 2172m intermediate station of the Sulden cable car, and return the same way – allow at least 4hr.

At **Sulden** (1860m), at the rear of Hotel Eller and close to the old **church**, is the start of path n.3. It winds uphill S through beautiful larch woods, the only shady section of the day, and passes under the chairlift a couple of times. Ignore all turn-offs (unless you want to take the steep Wurzelweg shortcut, announced by a friendly wooden gnome sculpture). Emerging from the wood, you traverse rocky meadows at the foot of a grey moraine ridge, the first of many today. A swing NW brings you to the **Langenstein chairlift** and café (2330m, 1hr 30min), with

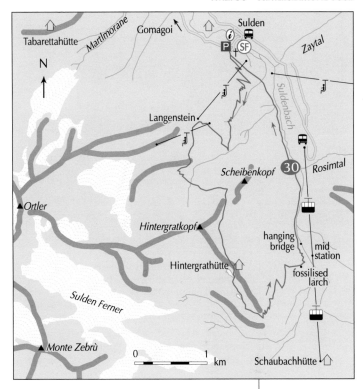

wonderful views east to the Zay and Rosim valleys separated by the Vertain Spitz.

Continue on n.3 – the Morosini Weg – S across the lunar terrain of the waves of moraine, bulldozed for winter skiing here. The path narrows a little around the corner below the tongues of the 'End der Welt' (End of the World) glacier. Yellow Rhaetian poppies brighten the way as you traverse into a neighbouring valley, and older white-grey moraine is consolidated by plants such as mountain avens and saxifrages. Moving SE onto grassy terrain with marmot burrows, the way steepens en route towards the rocky corner of **Scheibenkopf**. Still climbing

At Hintergrathütte

and mostly S from here on, it narrows, becoming more dramatic and moderately exposed. Across red rock under **Hintergratkopf** the path runs fantastically high over the upper Sulden valley, aided by lengths of cable. You finally cross to the R of the crest and all difficulty is forgotten as a breathtaking spectacle presents itself. Only steps away stands **Hintergrathütte** (2661m, 1hr 30min) in a superb amphitheatre housing a lake and bounded by Königspitze/Gran Zebrù and Monte Zebrù and their spectacular ice cascades. To the south are Suldenspitze and neighbours, as well as Schaubachhütte. ◄

Treat yourself to lunch or a drink at the refuge to take it all in.

> The **Hintergrathütte** is delightful and old-style, and has been a crucial base for climbers since 1922. Its predecessor was the 1892 Baeckmann Hütte, named after a generous St Petersburg mountaineer who donated it to the Sulden guides.

Next, follow path n.2 past the lake and over the lip for a steady descent on rocky grassland, all the time alongside a huge moraine ridge originating from the Sulden glacier. Curving ENE you set your sights on the

The Langenstein chairlift

cable car station below, although it takes a while to get there. ▸ Ignore the fork R (2172m, 1hr) for the mid-station of the cable car and brace yourself for the exciting plunge N as the path finds its way down a near-vertical cliff 200m high. In places chains and cables help, as do steps. Never far away the **Suldenbach** crashes through a chasm, and can be admired from a nearby **hanging bridge**. But path n.2 sticks to the L bank, soon reaching gentler terrain and grazing cows. Past the fork R for the lower cable car and bus stop (1916m), proceed on n.7 in common with a Kulturpromenade, a stroll past artistic installations and the like, that delivers you back at the old church of Sulden (1860m, 1hr).

Make a short detour to admire a partially fossilised larch trunk ring-dated back to AD494, and submerged by the glacier in the 7th century.

WALK 31
Düsseldorferhütte and Kanzel Circuit

Start/Finish	Tourist office, Sulden
Distance	14.6km (9 miles)
Ascent/Descent	870m
Difficulty	Grade 1–2
Walking time	5hr
Access	Sulden/Solda has year-round SAD bus links via Gomagoi with Spondinig/Spondigna and trains.

A contender for title of Greatest Walk in the Stelvio National Park, this circuit rewards walkers with superb views to the majestic Ortler. The going is straightforward and suitable for family groups who may prefer to ease the ascent by riding the Kanzel chairlift both ways, carving around 2hr off the day's total. Lunch and refreshments are available at both the historic 1892 Düsseldorferhütte (built by the Alpine Club of Düsseldorf) and the Kanzel café.

From the **tourist office** at Sulden (1860m) walk down the road across the **Suldenbach** river and take the lane SE (not the minor road) diagonally up the other side through meadows. Alongside Villa Zai (next to Hotel Cristallo) you cross straight over the road up a lane to the Düsseldorferhütte car park. Here a wooden arrow points you up a lane, past another hotel and R to a helpful *punto panoramico* (viewpoint) equipped with mountain profiles and a huge set of binoculars.

Not far on, at a ski lift, do not cross the stream (the return route comes this way) but fork L (NE) on n.5 for the start of the climb up forested **Zaytal**. As the wood begins to thin, you cross the gushing stream to rocky meadows in the company of cows and marmots. Ignore turn-offs and keep up to the **2391m junction** (1hr 30min) where the Kanzel path joins up. The refuge can already be seen high above, and after a bridge crossing, a well-graded winding path makes its way NNE up grassed slopes, weaving through jumbles of broken rock splattered with green lichen.

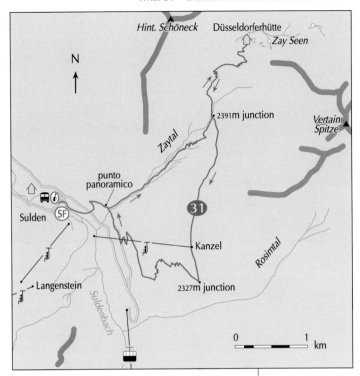

Düsseldorferhütte/Rifugio Serristori (2722m, 1hr) stands in a superb position near the Zay Seen lakes, a perfect belvedere for the Ortler and neighbours south-west, not to mention an awesome line-up at the rear of the hut: from Vertain Spitze southeast to Tschenglser Hochwand north-northeast. The building stands on a natural shelf of glacially smoothed rock alongside batches of roches moutonnées, so-called 'sheep rocks', while normal-sized live specimens graze among gentians, daisies and pink saxifrage cushions. The resident population of alpine choughs will also undoubtedly be out in force on the quest for crumbs. Time permitting, there is ample scope for exploration here.

The magnificent Ortler and Düsseldorferhütte

Appropriately rested and refreshed, descend the same way you came to the bridge and 2391m junction (40min) and fork L (due S) on n.12. This panoramic path coasts easily over terrain spread with cushions of wild thyme and creamy milfoil blooms. Huge rock slabs and trunk walkways are soon crossed as you leave the Zaytal and gain **Kanzel** (2348m, 30min) and chairlift. Continue past the café-restaurant through the gate and woodland dotted with Arolla pine sentinels and bushes of juniper.

At the next **junction** (2327m), a lovely spot with picnic benches, turn R and soon sharp L (W) for the zigzagging descent through the cool conifers of Malser Wald. At a fork (2041m) and bench turn R on n.15, a route with keep-fit installations. After crossing a lane it passes under the chairlift and soon curves L. Take care not to miss the marked path that soon breaks off R to join n.6 – go R past Hotel Zebrù for a short stretch to the opening of Zaytal where you resume the route followed on the opening stretch of the walk. Retrace your steps back to Sulden (1860m, 1hr 20min).

WALK 32
Madritschjoch and Hintere Schöntaufspitze

Start/Finish	Gasthof Enzian
Distance	14km (8.7 miles)
Ascent/Descent	1300m
Difficulty	Grade 2–3
Walking time	6hr 45min
Access	The road in upper Martelltal/Val Martello terminates at Gasthof Enzian where there are car parks and a bus stop for the summer SAD service.

A hefty climb but worth every metre and puff of the way to a glorious walkers' peak over the glaciated core of the Ortler-Cevedale group. Even if you cut the walk short and stop at 3123m Madritschjoch/Passo di Madriccio (200m lower and 1hr less), it makes a superbly memorable day out. Whatever you choose, it is advisable to defer the walk until mid–late summer as snow cover could hamper progress. The paths are clear and straightforward; only the last leg to the peak itself entails a little scrambling and exposure.

Both pass and peak are accessible with considerably less effort from the western side and Sulden – via the cable car to 2581m Schaubachhütte/Rifugio Città di Milano – however, on that approach the landscape is marred by ski lifts and pistes. Moreover the vision of Königspitze from the eastern approach as described here is something very special.

From the **Gasthof Enzian** bus stop (2055m) walk up the road past the Gasthof Schönblick fork and a kiosk to the well-signed turn-off R for n.150. The track climbs easily SW through a beautiful wood of larch, Arolla pine, juniper and alpenrose, crossing timber bridges over gushing streams. As the trees begin to thin and the wide way veers S, fork R (SW) at a signed junction on path n.151. This climbs towards a rock barrier where it is joined by a link from Zufallhütte/Rifugio Corsi. Branch R (NW) again for the continuing climb over a rise and into peaceful **Madritschtal** where up ahead is the magnificent view of Madritschspitz west-northwest.

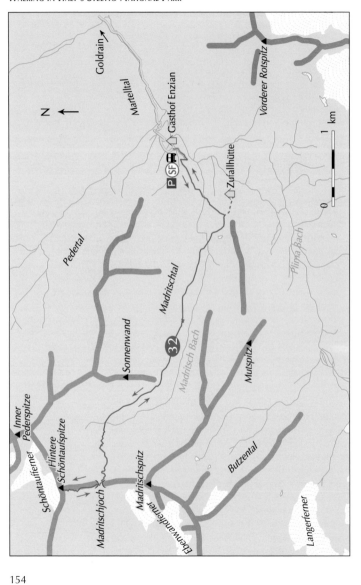

Stream crossing in Madritschtal

A flat marshy area is negotiated with stepping stones before a bridge crossing, then the clear path keeps up the right side of the valley, climbing steadily WNW. The grassy-rock terrain is home to marmots along with bright yellow alpine pasque flowers and pink primroses. It is a short climb to a second pasture flat and stream crossing by bridge. Then comes a steep shoulder where the path madly zigzags. Make the most of stops to catch your breath to admire the vast spreads of glacier south between Zufrittspitz and Cime Venezia.

Soon the angular shape of Sonnenwand dominates the path, marking a change of direction – NW now;

Grandiose views from Madritschjoch

your destinations, Hintere Schöntaufspitze flanked by the Madritschjoch, come into view northwest. At the 2800m mark the path heads W across a broad amphitheatre, where a stream trickles and snow lies late. Much steeper here, it is up via a rock platform for the final leg of ascent in tight zigzags to the ample saddle of **Madritschjoch** (3123m, 3hr 30min). You will be greeted by the stunning sight of Königspitze southwest and the Ortler northwest.

Turn R (due N) for the well-marked and trodden path that follows the left-hand side of the earth crest. The opening stretch is quite steep and crumbly, slippery in places, and necessitates extra care. However, the going levels out on the broad upper crest to **Hintere Schöntaufspitze** (3325m, 30min) where the wind plays strange games around the huge summit cairn. Of the fantastic spectacular 360° outlook, landmarks that stand out are the twin-pointed Cevedale (south), the Ortler (west-northwest), the Swiss Alps of the Engadine and even a pale spire or two of the Dolomites (east) if you are lucky.

The incontestable star of this walk, elegant slender **Königspitze/Gran Zebrù**, is breathtakingly sheer. A glacier tumbles down the impossible face, detouring the curious ice nose beneath the summit. The mountain's imposing shape is thought to be the reason for the German name 'king's summit', in stark contrast to the local belief that it was abode of the spirits of evil men! The Italian name comes from the valley to its north (see Walk 20). A 20-year old Franciscan friar Steinberger is thought to have been the first to scale it solo in 1854; in a similarly incredible vein, Austrian soldiers occupied the summit during WWI.

The descent gives you time to admire the upper Martelltal peaks

Return the same way to Madritschjoch (3123m, 30min), and the rest of the way down Madritschtal to Gasthof Enzian bus stop (2055m, 2hr 15min).

WALK 33
The Martelltal Glacier Trail

Start/Finish	Gasthof Enzian
Distance	11km (6.8 miles)
Ascent/Descent	750m
Difficulty	Grade 2
Walking time	4hr 15min
Access	The road in upper Martelltal/Val Martello terminates at Gasthof Enzian where there are car parks and a bus stop for the summer SAD service.

This is a wonderfully varied day's walk commencing in woodland and continuing across rock terrain with wide-ranging views to a host of glaciers and peaks including the majestic Cevedale and Königspitze. A fair amount of climbing and descending is involved, but the rewards are manifold. Two well-run refuges are visited, handy for drinks and meals, while self-catering walkers are spoilt for choice of perfect picnic spots. Moreover, thanks to the network of signed paths, there is plenty of room for mixing and matching, shortening or extending the route at will. A 'Gletscherlehrpfad/Sentiero Glaciologico' (glacier trail) is followed, and while it does not traverse any ice fields, it is punctuated with points of interest (P1, P2 and so on) testifying to the glaciers – at least double their present size – that occupied the valley 7000 years ago.

From the **Gasthof Enzian** bus stop (2055m) walk up the road past the Gasthof Schönblick fork and a kiosk to the well-signed turn-off R for the Gletscherlehrpfad/Sentiero Glaciologico. This is path n.150, a wide track that climbs easily SW through a beautiful wood of larch, Arolla pine, juniper and alpenrose, and across timber bridges over gushing streams. Before you know it, you have left the trees behind and are up at the superb terrace of glacially smoothed rock slabs occupied by **Zufallhütte/Rifugio Corsi P1** (2264m, 40min).

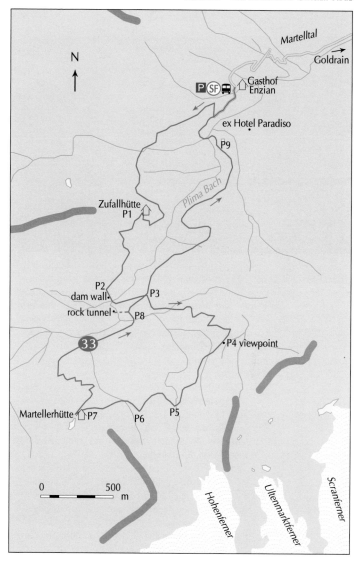

Approaching the dam wall, the Cevedale is visible

The **original 1882 refuge** was the work of the Dresden Alpine Club. Transferred to the Milano CAI branch and reconstructed in 1927, it was named for a leading mountaineer. It comes complete with a tiny WWI commemorative chapel and a ruined building, all that is left of an Austrian command post.

The twin Cevedale peaks are already visible southwest, as is Martellerhütte, but better is to come further up. Still straightforward, n.150 now leads S through meadows where marmots romp, over a glacial 'step' and to the late 19th-century **dam wall** (2318m, 20min, **P2**), rather incongruous nowadays.

The **drystone dam** was built in 1893 to prevent repeated mud and ice floods that would sweep down and devastate the lower villages. Legends supply a more colourful if not downright bizarre explanation for the catastrophes: the souls of virtuous women were said to migrate to the

Cevedale mountain and dwell there in ice palaces. These palaces collapsed dramatically during the frequent visits of Der Wilde, the 'wild man', sending the meltwater flooding dangerously downhill.

Nowadays, to prevent excessive build-up at the dam, the meltwater streams have been diverted and flow under the wall by way of an artificial rock tunnel, visited on the return stretch of the walk.

Turn L along the wall. For the time being ignore signs for Martellerhütte and keep on n.31A to **P3**, not far from the foot of a crashing waterfall swollen with the melting ice from the Hohenferner. Here fork R on n.37 and across a bridge for the start of a steady climb. The going is steepish, but tight zigzags ease the gradient up to a lunar rock terrace surprisingly bright with flowers, a minuscule lake and magnificent **viewpoint** (2550m, **P4**) with a beckoning bench. Soon comes a walk along the top of a moraine ridge before a fork R sees you at **P5** and the bridge across a rushing stream. ▶

The nearby moraine is newly formed as the Hohenferner/ Vedretta Alta above has shrunk markedly since an expansion in 1985.

Viewpoint at P4 on the glacier trail

On the way to Martellerhütte

A final short climb brings you to **P6**, in view of a yellow marker on a boulder used by the glaciological services for measuring purposes. Soon you round a point to cross broken rock before the short descent to **Martellerhütte/Rifugio Martello** (2610m, 1hr 30min, **P7**), a hospitable and comfortable hut built by the AVS in 1981. This is quite a spot, looking to immense glaciers with smooth ice humps and cracked crevasses spilling from the Cevedale. The orientation table helps put names to the multitude of peaks.

> The 'queen' of Martelltal is the **Cevedale**, a twin-peaked mountain that borders with the Trentino region of the Stelvio National Park. Its highest summit (3759m) is known as Monte Cevedale, while the other, Cime Cevedale (3752m), is better known as Zufallspitze, the ancient name used by the valley's inhabitants. The first ascents of the two peaks – by Payer with Pingger and Reinstadler, von Mojsisovics and Janiger – date back to 1864–65 and the mountain ranks as the third highest in the Ortler group.

The Gletscherlehrpfad/Sentiero Glaciologico – now n.103 – proceeds mostly N down the steep mountainside madly zigzagging to the valley floor, where it veers R (ENE) in the company of **Plima Bach**. The marshy terrain here was formed recently with material deposited by landslides and avalanches, and has since been colonised by multi-coloured masses of scented daphne and buttercups.

After a bridge over the Hohenferner waterfall stream, comes **P8** and wooden steps in descent. At the signed turn-off R, It is worthwhile taking 10min out for an interesting detour to the artificial **tunnel** under the dam wall: walk across the meadow to the fencing at the stream to see the rock tunnel and nearby, the dry river bed, the original course. Return the same way to the turn-off then walk over to the end of the dam wall and straight over (NE) for path n.40.

Soon there are giddy views into the sheer-sided canyon of Plima Bach then the path runs past a sea of waving white cotton grass and gradually returns to the cover of trees. Make sure you keep L on path n.37 to **P9** with a view of the red former Hotel Paradiso from the 1930s, now rapidly crumbling. Curving L you reach a pretty lake, a favourite with alpine swifts that skim the surface for insects. The way soon veers L onto a lane and bridge high over the torrent once more, then it is around to the car parks and Gasthof Enzian bus stop (2055m, 1hr 45min).

WALK 34
Zufritt See and Larchboden Loop

Start/Finish	Hotel Zum See
Distance	7.5km (4.6 miles)
Ascent/Descent	400m
Difficulty	Grade 1–2
Walking time	2hr 20min
Access	The road in upper Martelltal is served by the summer SAD bus service, which stops at the top end of the lake outside Hotel Zum See before continuing up to Gasthof Enzian.

This is a delightful and straightforward half-day walk that runs high along the southern side of Martelltal through beautiful woodland alive with woodpeckers, nutcrackers, squirrels and roe deer – not hard to see thanks to the scarcity of walkers. Well marked throughout, it begins at Zufritt See/Lago di Gioveretto, one of the area's high-altitude lakes dammed in the 1960s for hydroelectricity. It continues uphill to a hotel area where a detour is feasible for lunch. After a beautifully panoramic traverse it returns to the lakeside. If so desired, the opening uphill section can be avoided by taking the bus as far as Gasthof Enzian.

From the bus stop at **Hotel Zum See** (1864m) walk up the road past the car park and turn L following signs for n.36. This returns briefly to the road before heading off L again for a lovely stretch in the company of gushing **Plima Bach**. Soon it begins to climb in earnest away from the valley floor, and gaps in the trees offer exciting views to the river in a dramatic gorge of inclined slabs. Through a gate and over a rise, you reach the faded red former **Hotel Paradiso** (2088m) set on glacially smoothed rocks with lovely views upvalley to Zufallhütte and beyond. The path now flanks a marshy meadows of cotton grass before reaching a junction (50min) where the route from Gasthof Enzian joins up.

The lovely descent path looks over upper Martelltal

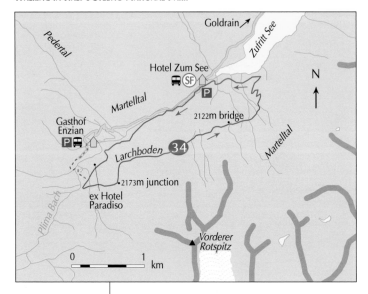

Access from Gasthof Enzian (15min)
From the bus stop (2055m) walk up the road past the car parks and kiosk, following waymarks for n.12. Ignore the popular fork right for Zufallhütte and keep on the lane for the bridge over Plima Bach. Not far up n.12 forks R past a pretty lake with skimming alpine swifts to the junction with n.36 in view of Hotel Paradiso.

Keep straight ahead, then at the junction fork L on n.12. This proceeds E uphill through thriving woods of larch and Arolla trees, bilberry, alpenrose and juniper shrubs. At a **2173m junction** are brilliant views W up Madritschtal/Val Madriccio and northwest up Pedertal/Val Peder. Keep L here for a lovely stretch through the area referred to as Larchboden between carpets of alpenrose and grassland spattered with marmot burrows amid rocks fallen from the rugged flanks of Vorderer Rotspitz/Cima Rossa di Martello. It is not far to a fork – go L on n.12A which follows a stream down to an idyllic pasture basin. Here the path crosses to the R side of the water-course – follow waymarks on rocks. The gentle descent continues through a sequence of meadows, and milky blue **Zufritt See** is soon glimpsed through the trees. At a **bridge** (2122m) keep L on n.12B to coast high above the lake to more bridges under a thundering waterfall. At last the path begins to descend in earnest, heading N and down past fencing. As a wider path is reached, fork L (n.17) down to the lakeside lane – turn L again to get back to Hotel Zum See (1864m, 1hr 30min).

Zufritt See can be seen through the trees

WALK 35
Stallwieshof Traverse

Start	Gasthof Enzian
Finish	Waldheim
Distance	14km (8.7 miles)
Ascent	600m
Descent	1100m
Difficulty	Grade 2+
Walking time	4hr 30min
Access	The road in upper Martelltal terminates at Gasthof Enzian where there are car parks and a bus stop for the SAD summer service. Waldheim also has a bus stop.

This highly recommended itinerary follows the northwest flank of Martelltal through woods with superbly scenic openings. For the most part it is straightforward, with a handful of exceptions: narrow sections of path after Lyfi Alm and a couple of elementary aided rock passages (ladders and handrail) after Rosimtal, all of which require due care and a sure foot along with stable good weather. Not many walkers come this way, improving chances of spotting wildlife. Scenic picnic places abound, and there are two family-managed farm-cum-guesthouses en route, Lyfi Alm and Stallwieshof – the latter has a deservedly high reputation for its local dishes and homemade cordials. The other farms are just huts with no facilities for walkers.

Lots of access/exit paths connecting with the main valley road and bus stops mean that variations are possible.

From the **Gasthof Enzian** bus stop (2055m) walk down the road a few minutes to the clutch of signposts and fork L uphill on the farm lane, n.39. This quickly reaches **Enzian Alm**, the site of the highest Advent market in the Alps. Continue on the wide forestry track over a bridge and cascading torrent. Easy curves lead through conifer wood heading essentially NE to **Lyfi Alm** (2165m, 50min). ◄

An exit route, n.10, descends to Zufritthaus and a bus stop on the roadside.

From here on, n.8 is a path, which goes across a stream and around the corner NE to meadows dotted

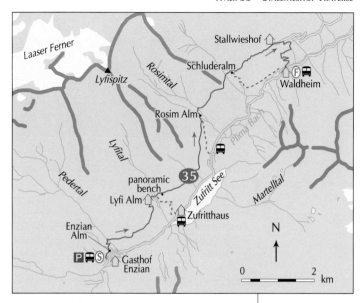

with black vanilla orchids and a perfectly placed **bench** overlooking pastel green Zufritt See, and wonderful views southwest to the Cevedale peaks and glacier extensions backing the upvalley refuges. Due east is Zufrittspitz/ Gioveretto and its ice and snow splattered neighbours. ▶

A short detour breaks off here to visit ancient larch trees 'Larici monumentali'.

Successive ups and downs continue NE through sweet smelling conifer woods alive with squawking nutcrackers that compete to be heard over the crashing of waterfalls from the opposite flanks of Martelltal. A wooden ladder descent and stream crossings precede a magnificent rock slab lookout over the dam wall of Zufritt See, while the down-valley view over strawberry fields and hillside farms extends as far north as the Similaun-Texel groups. Further abrupt descent is necessary to dip below a steep rock outcrop, before another short ladder then a fork (where n.9A forks R to drop to the road). Due N now comes an open stretch with a warning of 'possible rockfalls in rain', then it is uphill to join path

Enjoying the down-valley views

n.9 (from the road). This climbs up the bank of the gushing torrent in **Rosimtal** to cross it on a bridge R. Further ascent passes two huts to a wonderful clearing and path junction (2060m, 1hr 10min) looking up to beautiful Schluderspitze north-northwest.

Branch R (NE) to yet another lookout point before more descent, including a ladder and a steep passage down a rock face with stone steps and wooden handrail. Once on safe ground take time out to admire the plunging views to the valley floor as well as Stallwieshof and Waldheim, where you are headed. An abrupt curve L (N) and a final short aided stretch leads into the beautiful Schludertal, dominated by the imposing bastion of Schluderhorn northwest. Across the torrent are the timber huts of **Schluderalm** (2005m, 1hr). ◀

A path breaks off in direct descent to Waldheim bus stop from here.

The straightforward path coasts through woods, with two stretches signed as possibly subject to rockfalls, finally reaching alpine farm and inn **Stallwieshof** (1931m, 40min).

Duly restored, take the road away from the buildings and past a 350-year old watermill. Very soon path n.5 forks off R, down to a minor road. Here it swings sharp S via a string of huts, following a perfectly graded old route that cuts down the increasingly steep conifer-forested mountainside in wide curves. It finally emerges on the valley floor to cross Plima Bach to **hotel-café Waldheim** (1521m, 50min).

WALK 36
Pedertal

Start/Finish	Gasthof Enzian
Distance	12km (7.4 miles)
Ascent/Descent	630m
Difficulty	Grade 2
Walking time	3hr 30min
Access	The road in upper Martelltal terminates at Gasthof Enzian where there are car parks and a bus stop for the summer SAD service.

Undeniably one of the best walks in Martelltal – and indeed the Stelvio National Park as a whole – this is rewarding and not too strenuous. It explores beautiful, little visited Pedertal/Val Peder, home to chamois, marmots and birds of prey, before embarking on a panoramic traverse that showcases the entire line-up of mountains and glaciers that form the valley's south-southeast edge. Take a picnic lunch unless you plan on tasting the traditional culinary delights at Lyfi Alm, located towards the end of the walk.

From the **Gasthof Enzian** bus stop (2055m) walk down the road for a couple of minutes to the lane forking L signed for n.20 and others. A short way up is the **Enzian Alm** summer farm, and immediately after the building you need to turn L on n.20. The clear path climbs steadily through the wood alive with squirrels. A couple of streams are crossed then after a rise, the way veers R and down to a bridge over a cascading torrent. Up the other side you join a wider path and go L (NW) up **Pedertal**, with a gentler gradient. Arolla pines and juniper are dominant, but the trees soon thin considerably to give way to flowered grassland in a beautiful river plain. Further up the stream is crossed twice on bridges, before you reach a junction and picnic table alongside the heap of stones that mark the spot of the former **Schildhütte** (2415m, 1hr 15min, incorrectly located on commercial maps).

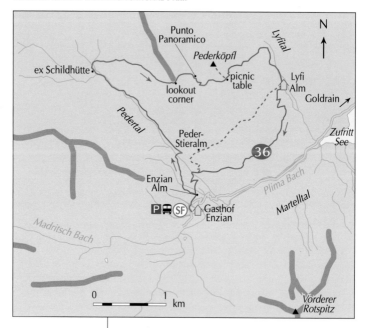

Fork R (E) across two streams for a gentle ascent to a path fork, where you keep straight ahead (SE) on n.33. There are lovely views around upper Pedertal, beset with cirques and rugged peaks, but better is to come. You gradually coast up to a **lookout corner** (2581m) where a picnic table has been wisely placed. Now you can take in the immense line-up opposite that goes from Zufrittspitz/ Gioveretto (east) all the way via glaciers and moraines galore to Cevedale (southwest).

When you can drag yourself away, there is a short descent to an official punto panoramico with all the peaks named on an orientation table. The path continues downhill R (SE) to coast through a veritable garden with a high concentration of black vanilla orchids and purple asters before rounding the foot of the Pederköpfl. Near a junction is another superbly placed **picnic table**, this time with especially grandiose views to the Cevedale.

Pederköpfl (30min return)
If by chance you have not yet had your fill of views, by all means take time to clamber up to the 2585m top of **Pederköpfl**; a faint path strikes out NW from the picnic table.

The descent proceeds NE, the clear path threading its way through broken rocks brightened with flowers, to reach the **Lyfital** and its stream (2323m). Above on the slopes, Arolla pines stand like sentinels, while the views range southeast to magnificent cirques beneath Sallent Spitze and Zufrittspitz. Go R into the wood and down to **Lyfi Alm** (2165m, 1hr 30min). The final leg follows an easy farm lane SW, looping through woodland, back down to Enzian Alm and from there to the Gasthof Enzian bus stop (2055m, 45min).

Variant return
With a little extra effort, it is worth embarking on an extra 100m in ascent by following path n.35 to **Peder-Stieralm** (2252m), old huts with drinking water and benches for admiring more incredible views. Then take n.39, which plunges to join the farm lane from Lyfi Alm. Turn R and follow it back to the Gasthof Enzian bus stop (2055m, 1hr).

At Peder-Stieralm

WALK 37

Orgelspitze

Start/Finish	Stallwieshof
Distance	10km (6.2 miles)
Ascent/Descent	1370m
Difficulty	Grade 3
Walking time	6hr 30min
Access	A year-round SAD bus runs to Martell/Martello but it is a further 6km on a surfaced road to Stallwieshof. Walkers without cars can always use the local taxi (Tel 335 7724607).

Towering from the northern edge of Martelltal is 3305m high Laaser Spitz or Punta di Lasa, known locally as Orgelspitze (any of the three names are used on commercial maps). Despite the intimidating length of the ascent – nearly 1400m – any experienced and fit walker can handle the climb in good conditions. Mid-late summer and autumn are preferable for optimum visibility and to ensure potentially dangerous ice has melted and the new season's snowfalls not yet begun. Waymarking is clear and frequent and the path trouble-free until the final 350m when it becomes steeper, rougher and entails some clambering but no exposure. All effort is more than adequately rewarded as the extensive panoramas are breathtaking. Do not forget to record your visit in the ascent book stored in a box on the summit cross.

Stallwieshof at the start of the walk is a lovely place to stay and eat.

From **Stallwieshof** (1931m) walk along the road to the path junction near the 350-year-old watermill where you are pointed L (NW) on n.5. The path soon enters a wood of Arolla pine and larch, with juniper and alpenrose shrubs on open terrain. Little time is spent on zigzags and the path climbs straight up grassy banks studded with stemless carline thistles. Ignore turn-offs and keep on through hollows lined with bilberry plants which turn bright red in late summer. A fresh **spring** marks the 2200m level; soon n.5 bears L (W) leaving the trees behind for a desolate valley, its scattered stones green with lichen. A long climb ensues via terraces where sheep graze on

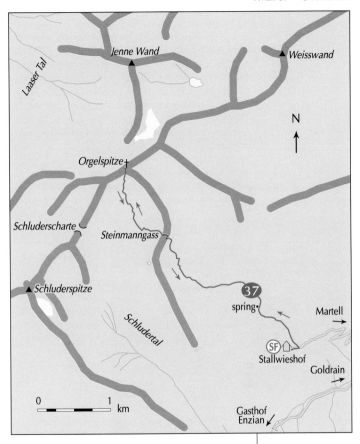

ever-barer terrain, waymarking mostly cairns with red/ white paint splashes.

Around the 2900m level you come to a pillar-like cairn and enter yet another upper valley, this one flatter, virtually a plateau and often snowbound well into summer. This is the Steinmanngass, a curious sight, its stone detritus base appearing steamrollered. Due west now is the Schluderscharte, a weathered dip in the crumbly rock strata angled at 45°, beyond which rise pyramidal tips in the Vertain-Hohe Angelus group. Not far on, the Orgelspitze itself comes into sight.

The remaining 300m is where the going gets rougher, on steeper, tiring terrain that involves clambering over rock debris. You eventually approach a saddle for the final puff to the spectacular summit of **Orgelspitze** (3305m, 4hr). At your feet stretches Vinschgau/Val Venosta, surrounded by a high-altitude 360° panorama of mountains: from east anti-clockwise are the Dolomites, Grossglockner, Similaun and Weisskugel, then the multitudinous summits of the Ortler-Cevedale range. From the summit itself the ridge extending northwards terminates in the Jenne Wand, an unusually light colour due to its marble composition.

On the top of Orgelspitze

The name **Orgelspitze** is a derivation of the ancient 'Arge' meaning 'evil' as signs of approaching bad weather are first manifest on this mountain. It has long been visited by the valley inhabitants who heaped up the colossal stone pillar-cairn on the summit as a beacon.

Watching your step, return the same way to Stallwieshof (1931m, 2hr 30min).

WALK 38
Soyalm

Start/Finish	Hölderle Café
Distance	4.8km (2.9 miles)
Ascent/Descent	600m
Difficulty	Grade 1–2
Walking time	3hr 30min
Access	The summer SAD bus bound for Gasthof Enzian in upper Martelltal stops outside Hölderle Café. Otherwise allow 30min on foot (path n.36) for the 2km from Gand where the year-round bus arrives.

Martelltal is a beautiful, laidback valley where the timber and livestock activities are as important as outdoor tourism. The destination of this walk, Soyalm, is a working farm located high above the valley floor at 2072m, and accessible solely on foot. Occupied throughout the summer months, it is managed by a local family who decided many years back to branch out and open the premises to visitors, so the place is now a well-reputed Jausenstation, eatery-cum-café. The relatively short access makes this walk suitable for everyone whose comfort zone embraces a 600m height difference. The farm's location is of course beautiful, on the edge of woodland dominated by larch trees, with lovely views that take in the moraine spread below the Soyferner and the monumental Zufrittspitz/Gioveretto.

Alongside **Hölderle Café** (1457m) is signposted path n.4 which heads uphill SE through beautiful conifer forest carpeted with bilberry shrubs. A wide track is soon joined and the climb proceeds in wide zigzags towards a waterfall, although this is only glimpsed. ▶ Around halfway up, a cascading torrent is crossed, then a wide pasture corridor leads up out of the trees and due E beneath the Elferspitz to the buildings of **Soyalm** (2072m, 2hr), a delightful spot where a tranquil herd of caramel-coloured horses graze alongside contented cows.

This flank of the valley is shady and damp, perfect conditions for the mushrooms and fungus that thrive here.

Afterwards return to the roadside the same way you came, to Hölderle Café (1457m, 1hr 30min).

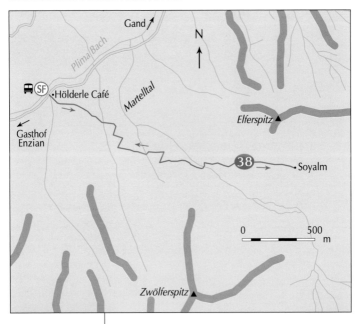

At Soyalm

APPENDIX A
Route summary table

Walk	Title	Time	Distance	Ascent/Descent	Grade	Page
1	St Gertraud Alm route	5hr 10min	14.5km (9 miles)	700m/700m	1–2	37
2	Höchsterhütte Circuit	4hr 30min	14km (8.7 miles)	700m/700m	2	41
3	Fischersee Walk	2hr	6km (3.7 miles)	200m/200m	2	46
4	Rifugio Lago Corvo	5hr 20min	11.5km (7.1 miles)	1050m/1050m	2	49
5	Rifugio Dorigoni Tour	6hr 30min	18km (11 miles)	1200m/1200m	2	54
6	Baito Campisolo Route	5hr 15min	11km (6.8 miles)	800m/800m	2	59
7	Cascate di Saent	2hr 10min	6km (3.7 miles)	350m/350m	1	63
8	Ragaiolo Falls and the Venetian Sawmill	1hr 30min	4.5km (2.8 miles)	230m/230m	1–2	66
9	Val Cercen	3hr	10km (6.2 miles)	500m/500m	1–2	69
10	Rifugio Larcher Tour	5hr	13.5km (8.4 miles)	750m/750m	2	72
11	Monte Vioz	6hr 30min	14.5km (9 miles)	1330m/1330	3	77
12	Sentiero dei Tedeschi	5hr	16.5km (10.3 miles)	365m/1275m	2–3	82

179

Walk	Title	Time	Distance	Ascent/Descent	Grade	Page
13	Malga Covel and Waterfalls	3hr 20min	14km (8.7 miles)	700m/700m	1–2	87
14	Forte Barba di Fior Loop	3hr 20min	11km (6.8 miles)	500m/500m	2	91
15	Lago di Pian Palù Circuit	3hr 15min	10km (6.2 miles)	440m/440m	1	93
16	Dosso Tresero	3hr 40min	10.5km (6.5 miles)	650m/650m	1–2	97
17	The Forni Sentiero Glaciologico Alto	3hr 20min	9km (5.6 miles)	600m/600m	1–2	100
18	Valle di Cedèc	3hr 30min	10.7km (6.6 miles)	550m/550m	1	104
19	Rifugio Casati	3hr 30min	8km (5 miles)	560m/560m	2–3	107
20	Val Zebrù and Rifugio V° Alpini	4hr 30min	9.2km (5.7 miles)	750m/750m	2–3	109
21	Lago della Manzina	3hr 40min	9km (5.6 miles)	610m/610m	1–2	113
22	Santa Caterina to Sant'Antonio	5hr 40min	17km (10.6 miles)	650m/1050m	1–2	116
23	Monte delle Scale	3hr	5km (3 miles)	570m/570m	1–2	120
24	Valle Forcola Traverse	3hr 30min	12km (7.5 miles)	300m/900m	1–2	123
25	Monte Scorluzzo and Filone dei Mòt	3hr 30min	9km (5.6 miles)	350m/850m	3	127

Walk	Title	Time	Distance	Ascent/Descent	Grade	Page
26	Goldseeweg	4hr 10min	14km (8.7 miles)	100m/1350m	2	132
27	Berglhütte	4hr	12.5km (7.7 miles)	645m/645m	1–2	136
28	Trafoi Waterfalls	2hr 50min	7.5km (4.6 miles)	250m/250m	1–2	140
29	Tabarettahütte	4hr 15min	9km (5.6 miles)	700m/700m	1–2	143
30	Hintergrathütte Tour	5hr	15km (9.3 miles)	850m/850m	2–3	146
31	Düsseldorferhütte and Kanzel Circuit	5hr	14.6km (9 miles)	870m/870m	1–2	150
32	Madritschjoch and Hintere Schöntaufspitze	6hr 45min	14km (8.7 miles)	1300m/1300m	2–3	153
33	The Martelltal Glacier Trail	4hr 15min	11km (6.8 miles)	750m/750m	2	158
34	Zufritt See and Larchboden Loop	2hr 20min	7.5km (4.6 miles)	400m/400m	1–2	164
35	Stallwieshof Traverse	4hr 30min	14km (8.7 miles)	600m/1100m	2+	168
36	Pedertal	3hr 30min	12km (7.4 miles)	630m/630m	2	171
37	Orgelspitze	6hr 30min	10km (6.2 miles)	1370m/1370m	3	174
38	Soyalm	3hr 30min	4.8km (2.9 miles)	600m/600m	1–2	177

APPENDIX B
Glossary

Italian	German	English
acqua (non) potabile	*(kein) Trinkwasser*	(un)drinkable water
agriturismo	*Jausenstation*	farm that serves meals
aiuto!	*zu Hilfe!*	help!
alta via	*Hohenweg*	high-level trek
altipiano, altopiano	*Hochebene*	high-level plateau
alto/basso, sopra/sotto	*ober/unten*	upper/lower
aperto/chiuso	*geöffnet/geschlossen*	open/closed
autostrada	*Autobahn*	motorway subject to toll
baita	*Alm*	alpine farm
bivacco	*Biwak*	unmanned hut for mountaineers
bocchetta, passo	*Joch, Scharte*	mountain pass
bosco	*Wald*	woodland
cabinovia, telecabina	*Umlaufbahn*	gondola lift
cantoniera		road maintenance building
capitello	*Wegkreuz*	shrine
cascata	*Wasserfall*	waterfall
caserma	*Kaserne*	barracks
castello	*Schloss*	castle
cengia	*Band*	ledge
cima, piz, vetta	*Gipfel, Spitze*	mountain peak
collegamento	*Verbindung*	link
coston	*Grat*	ridge
croce	*Kreuz*	cross
destra/sinistra	*rechts/links*	right/left
diga	*Staumauer*	dam
dormitorio	*Lager*	dormitory
fermata	*Haltestelle*	bus stop
fiume	*Fluß*	river
fontana	*Brunnen*	fountain
fonti, terme	*Bad*	spa
forcella	*Scharte*	mountain pass for walkers
funivia	*Seilbahn*	cable car
galleria	*Tunnel*	tunnel

Italian	German	English
gestore del rifugio	Huttenwirt	hut warden
ghiaccio	Eis	ice
ghiacciaio	Gletscher	glacier
giro	Rundgang	circuit
lago	See	lake
locanda	Gasthof	guesthouse
malga	Alm	high-altitude summer farm
monte, montagna	Berg	mountain
navetta	Pemdelverkehr	shuttle bus
nevaio	Firnfeld	firn, snowfield
ometto	Steinmann	cairn
orario	Fahrplan	timetable
paese	Dorf	village
pala, palon		steep mountain
panificio, fornaio	Bäkerei	bakery
pericolo	Gefahr	danger
ponte	Brücke	bridge
punto	Punkt	point, place
previsioni del tempo	Wettervorhersage	weather forecast
rifugio	Hütte	manned mountain hut
rio, torrente	Bach	stream
ristoro	Jausenstation	mountain café, restaurant
ruderi, rovine	Ruinen	ruins
scorciatoia	Abkürzung	shortcut
seggiovia	Sessellift	chairlift
sella	Sattel	saddle
sentiero	Weg, Steig	path, route
sorgente	Quelle	spring
stazione ferroviaria	Bahnhof	railway station
teleferica	Materialseilbahn	goods cableway
torre	Turm	tower
val, valle	Tal	valley
vedretta	Ferner	hanging glacier
via ferrata	Klettersteig	aided climbing route

APPENDIX C

Accommodation

Moderately priced suggestions for where to sleep in the towns and villages of the Stelvio National Park are given here. For complete lists, including self-catering options, contact the relevant tourist offices listed in Appendix D.

Hotels and B&Bs
Bormio
B&B Vecchio Borgo Tel 0342 904447

Cancano
Chalet Villa Valania Tel 0342 919434 www.chaletvillavalania.it

Gomagoi
Hotel Gallia Tel 0473 611773 www.hotel-gallia.it

Malè
Albergo Pensione Pangrazzi Tel 0463 901277 Email pensionepangrazzi@libero.it

Peio
Albergo Centrale Tel 0463 753244 www.albergocentralepeio.com

Peio Fonti
Hotel Europa Tel 0463 753133 www.hoteleuropa.tn.it

Rabbi Fonti
Grand Hotel Tel 0463 983050 www.grandhotelrabbi.it
Affittacamere Al Molin Tel 0463 985020 www.almolin.it
Albergo al Fontanin (Còler) Tel 0463 984017 www.alfontanin.it

Santa Caterina Valfurva
Hotel Compagnoni Tel 0342 925105 www.compagnoni.net

Sulden/Solda
Pension Dangl Tel 0473 613016 www.dangl-sulden.com

St Gertraud/Santa Geltrude
Ultnerhof Tel 0473 798117 www.ultnerhof.com

Stilfser Joch/Passo dello Stelvio
Berggasthof Tibet Tel 0342 903360 www.tibet-stelvio.com

Trafoi
Hotel Post 0473 612411 www.posthoteltrafoi.it

Martelltal/Val Martello
Gasthof Enzian Tel 0473 744755 www.gasthof-enzian.it

Lyfi Alm Tel 333 2770100 www.lyfialm.it
Stallwieshof Tel 0473 744552 www.stallwies.com

Campsites
Goldrain/Coldrano (Vinschgau/Val Venosta)
Camping Cevedale Tel 0473 742132 www.camping-cevedale.com

Isolaccia, Valdidentro (8km west of Bormio)
La Pineta Tel 0342 985365 www.campinglapineta-valdidentro.it

Peio
Val di Sole Camping Tel 0463 753177 www.valdisolecamping.it

Plan near Rabbi Fonti
Campeggio al Plan Tel 339 6699248 www.campeggiovaldirabbi.it

The approach to Stallwieshof (Walk 35)

Prad/Prato (Vinschgau/Val Venosta)
Camping Kiefernhain Tel 0473 616422 www.camping-kiefernhain.it

Trafoi
Camping Trafoi Tel 0473 611533 www.camping-trafoi.com

Mountain huts

Berglhütte/Rifugio Borletti Tel 338 3877344 www.berglhuette.it, early June to mid-October

Rifugio Branca Tel 0342 935501 www.rifugiobranca.it, March to September

Rifugio Campo Tel 0342 929185, late June to mid-September

Rifugio Casati Tel 0342 935507 www.rifugiocasati.it, end June to end September

Rifugio Dorigoni Tel 0463 985107 www.rifugiodorigoni.it, late June to late September

Rifugio Doss dei Cembri Tel 0463 753227 www.dossdeigembri.it, late June to mid-September

Düsseldorferhütte/Rifugio Serristori Tel 0473 613115 www.duesseldorferhuette.com, June to early October

Rifugio Garibaldi Tel 0342 904312 www.rifugiogaribaldi.it, June to October

Rifugio Ghiacciaio dei Forni Tel 0342 935365 www.forni2000.com, March to September

Hintergrathütte/Rifugio Coston Tel 0473 613188, mid-June to early October

Höchsterhütte/Rifugio Canziani Tel 0473 798120 www.ultental.it/hoechsterhuette, early June to end October

Rifugio Lago Corvo Tel 0463 985175, late June to late September

Rifugio Larcher al Cevedale Tel 0463 751770 www.rifugiocevedale.it, late June to late September

Rifugio Mantova al Vioz Tel 0463 751386 www.rifugiovioz.it, late June to mid-September

Payerhütte/Rifugio Payer Tel 0473 613010 www.payerhuette.com, end June to early October

Rifugio Pizzini Tel 0342 935513 www.rifugiopizzini.it, March to September

Rifugio V° Alpini Tel 0342 929170 www.rifugioquintoalpini.it, mid-June to mid-September

Schaubachhütte/Rifugio Città di Milano Tel 0473 613002 www.schaubachhuette.it, mid-June to mid-October

Tabarettahütte/Rifugio Tabaretta Tel 347 2614872 www.tabaretta.com, mid-June to mid-October

Zufallhütte/Rifugio N Corsi Tel 0473 744785 www.zufallhuette.com, mid-June to October

APPENDIX D
Useful contacts

Tourist information offices
Bormio Tel 0342 903300 www.bormio.eu, www.aptbormio.it
Cogolo Tel 0463 754345 www.promoturpejo.it, www.valdisole.net
Malé Tel 0463 900862 www.valdisole.net
Martelltal/Val Martello and Latsch/Laces Tel 0473 623109 www.laces-martello.com
Peio Tel 0463 753100 www.promoturpejo.it, www.valdisole.net
San Bernardo, Val di Rabbi Tel 0463 985048 www.valdirabbi.com, www.valdisole.net
Santa Caterina Valfurva Tel 0342 935544 www.santacaterina.it
St Walburg/San Valburga, Ultental/Val d'Ultimo Tel 0473 795387 www.ultental.it
Sulden/Solda Tel 0473 613015 www.ortlergebiet.it

Extra information
Alta Valtellina www.altavaltellina.eu (English version available)
Südtirol www.sentres.com (Italian and German)

Park visitor centres
Bormio Tel 0342 901654
Cogolo (Peio) Tel 0463 754186
Martell Tel 0473 745027 www.culturamartell.com
Rabbi Tel 0463 985190
St Gertraud/St Geltrude Tel 0473 798123 www.lahnersaege.com
Trafoi Tel 0473 612031 www.naturatrafoi.com

Local transport
Austrian Rail Tel www.oebb.at
Ferrovia Trento Malè and Trentino Trasporti Tel 0461 821000 www.ttesercizio.it
Paris Ultental Reisen Tel 0473 791013 www.ultental-reisen.it
Perego buses Tel 0342 701200 www.busperego.com
SAD Tel 840 000471 www.sad.it
Südtirol transport www.sii.bz.it
Trenitalia Tel 898021 www.trenitalia.com
Trenord Tel 800 500 005 www.trenord.it

Lifts
Sulden lifts www.seilbahnensulden.it

Taxis
Bormio Tel 0342 903768
Martell Tel 335 7724607
Peio Tel 338 3685394
Rabbi Tel 0463 985402
Trafoi Tel 0473 611704

LISTING OF CICERONE GUIDES

For full information on all
our guides, and to order
books and eBooks, visit our
website:
www.cicerone.co.uk.

Walking – Trekking – Mountaineering – Climbing – Cycling

Over 40 years, Cicerone have built up an outstanding collection of 300 guides, inspiring all sorts of amazing adventures.

Every guide comes from extensive exploration and research by our expert authors, all with a passion for their subjects. They are frequently praised, endorsed and used by clubs, instructors and outdoor organisations.

All our titles can now be bought as **e-books** and many as iPad and Kindle files and we will continue to make all our guides available for these and many other devices.

Our website shows any **new information** we've received since a book was published. Please do let us know if you find anything has changed, so that we can pass on the latest details. On our **website** you'll also find some great ideas and lots of information, including sample chapters, contents lists, reviews, articles and a photo gallery.

It's easy to keep in touch with what's going on at Cicerone, by getting our monthly **free e-newsletter**, which is full of offers, competitions, up-to-date information and topical articles. You can subscribe on our home page and also follow us on **Facebook** and **Twitter**, as well as our **blog**.

Cicerone – the very best guides for exploring the world.

CICERONE

2 Police Square Milnthorpe Cumbria LA7 7PY
Tel: 015395 62069 info@cicerone.co.uk
www.cicerone.co.uk